JOB BIBLE STUDY

UNLOCK THE DRAMA OF FAITH, FRIENDS, AND
FRUSTRATION

40-DAY BIBLE STUDY SERIES
BOOK 5

PETER DEHAAN

Job Bible Study: Unlock the Drama of Faith, Friends, and Frustration

© 2020, 2022, 2025 by Peter DeHaan.

40-Day Bible Study Series, book 5 (formerly *I Hope in Him & Dear Theophilus Job*)

Scriptures taken from the Holy Bible, New International Version®, NIV®. Copyright © 1973, 1978, 1984, 2011 by Biblica, Inc.™ Used by permission of Zondervan. All rights reserved worldwide. www.zondervan.com The "NIV" and "New International Version" are trademarks registered in the United States Patent and Trademark Office by Biblica, Inc.™

Library of Congress Control Number: 2025912029

Published by Rock Rooster Books

ISBN:

- e-book:979-8-88809-157-9
- paperback:979-8-88809-158-6
- hardcover:979-8-88809-159-3
- audiobook: 979-8-88809-160-9

Credits:

- Developmental editor: Cathy Rueter
- Copyeditor: Robyn Mulder
- Cover design: Fanderclai Design
- Author photo: Chelsie Jensen Photography

To Colton

40-Day Bible Study Series takes a fresh and practical look into Scripture, book by book.

Bible Character Sketches Series celebrates people in Scripture, from the well-known to the obscure.

Holiday Celebration Devotional Series rejoices in the holidays with Jesus.

Visiting Churches Series takes an in-person look at church practices and traditions to inform and inspire today's followers of Jesus.

Be the first to hear about Peter's new books and receive updates at PeterDeHaan.com/updates.

CONTENTS

THE BOOK OF JOB

Many people struggle reading the book of Job. Given that it's mostly dialogue, what may help is to consider Job as an early version of a screenplay. I, for one, would love to see Job turned into a stage production or a movie.

As we read Job, let's pretend we're reading a play or watching a movie. With the characters' conversations to guide us, we can imagine the setting, the drama, and the emotion. Here are the key things we need to know.

The story of Job has eight key characters:

- Job, the protagonist.

- God, Job's protector and overseer.
- Satan, Job's antagonist.
- Job's unsupportive wife, a bit part, albeit a painful one.
- Job's main friends: Eliphaz, Bildad, and Zophar. With friends like these, who needs enemies?
- Job's younger friend, Elihu, initially quiet and then opinionated.

The book of Job opens with a prologue (chapters 1 and 2) to establish the setting of the story. What occurs in the next 39 chapters (Job 3 through 41) is 99 percent dialogue, mostly between Job and his four increasingly critical friends.

The book of Job concludes with an epilogue (chapter 42) that supplies a satisfying ending. Aside from a brief conclusion by Job in the epilogue, the last significant words we have in our story come from God. It's fitting that God has the final word—and wise that Job listens.

In what ways does God speak to us? How open are we to listen to what he says?

[Discover more about listening to God in Psalm 85:8.]

DAY 1: ABOUT JOB
JOB 1:1–5

This man was blameless and upright; he feared God and shunned evil. Job 1:1

We open our story of Job by establishing the setting.

Job lives in the land of Uz (not Oz). But before we make the jump and assume this is a fairytale location, we should note that Jeremiah mentions Uz as a real place.

We learn four key things about Job.

First, Job is a righteous man. This means he's a good guy. He acts justly in all he does and conducts himself with blame-free confidence. He puts God first and avoids evil of all kinds. He's an example worth emulating.

Next, Job is a family man. He and his wife have ten kids. Though this may seem like an overwhelming number to most of us today, it's not to Job. In Bible times people saw children as a sure sign of God's favor. The more the better—a quiver full of them.

Job also carries concern for his kids and their future. After they party, which they do often, Job offers a sacrifice—a burnt offering—for each one of them. This is to purify them of any sin or careless thought. He does this because he wants to help make them right with God.

Last, Job is rich. He owns over 10,000 animals, with a large staff to oversee his herds. He is the wealthiest guy in the area, highly esteemed by all.

In short, Job enjoys an idyllic life of ease and favor from God. Surely, everyone looks up to Job and wants to be like him. This is how our unidentified narrator describes Job.

We might say Job's life is perfect, and so might he.

This is how our story begins. But like every story worth telling, we know that something will change, or else we won't have a story.

Before we read on, let's consider how Job's life compares to ours. We may be righteous, or we may fall short. We may have a large family, or we may have none. We may be prosperous, or we may have little. We may have the respect of others, or they may ignore us. Or we may fall somewhere in the middle of these extremes.

How do others see us? How does God view us? What needs to change?

[Discover more about another man, Noah, who was blameless and upright in Genesis 6:9.]

DIG DEEPER: TWO QUESTIONS ABOUT JOB

All Scripture is God-breathed and is useful for teaching, rebuking, correcting and training in righteousness.
2 Timothy 3:16

Today, some people debate the authenticity of Job. They question if he was a real person or if the book about him is a work of fiction.

Here are the indications that Job *wasn't* a real person: He doesn't appear in any of the historical books of the Bible. And he only receives mention in two other books in Scripture outside of the one that bears his name. Last, the Bible says that righteous

Job was without blame, which implies he never sinned. Since only God is sinless, this characterization is false—although it could also be hyperbole, a literary practice to make a point that occurs throughout the Bible.

However, there are also indications that Job *was* a real person: God, as recorded by the prophet Ezekiel, refers to Job along with Daniel and Noah. Surely, if Job were fictional, God would not mention him in the same context as these other two. In that same passage, God testifies that Job was righteous. It seems unlikely that God would so affirm a fictitious person.

So was Job a real person or not? Is his story fact or fiction?

We'll never resolve the answers to these questions, but it doesn't matter. Whether he is fact or fiction, Job's story is part of God's inspired word. That means we can learn from it, receive inspiration, and strengthen our faith because of it. Arguing if Job was real is only a distraction from the truth that the book holds.

Another question: When was the book of Job written? Some think Job was an early book of the Bible—perhaps even the first. They place him as a contemporary of Abraham. But this is mostly conjecture.

Regarding the timeline, consider these two observations. First, there are significant thematic parallels between the books of Job and Ecclesiastes, specifically about the brevity of life and futility of living. Second, the books of Job and Song of Songs have a similar construction, which doesn't appear anywhere else in the Bible. Each is heavy in dialogue—almost exclusively so—reading like a screenplay.

King Solomon wrote both Song of Songs and Ecclesiastes. Because the book of Job shares a similar construction to the Song of Songs and a parallel theme to Ecclesiastes, could Solomon have also written Job? This is mere speculation, but it's a thought to consider.

But, like our first question regarding whether Job was a real person, knowing when the book of Job took place, or who wrote it, doesn't really matter. What matters are the lessons we can learn from him.

Do we really expect that we can learn from all of Scripture?

[Discover more about Job in Ezekiel 14:14, 20 and James 5:11.]

DAY 2: GOD AND SATAN, PART 1
JOB 1:6–12

"Have you considered my servant Job? There is no one on earth like him." Job 1:8

Imagine the opening scene of our movie based on the book of Job. Father God sits on his throne in heaven, a grand station of authority adorned with ornate gold etchings. The light glimmers off it. But that's nothing compared to the aura of God's face that beams brightness in all directions. His chair sits elevated at the end of a spacious hall, massive white pillars aligning the passage. Open windows provide a gentle breeze, while supernatural songbirds fill the air with their praise.

Angels make their way to his grand throne, worshiping their creator and awaiting his instructions for the day. They shimmer with anticipation of their assignments and the critical role they will play to advance his kingdom.

But in their midst, one stands out of place. Dressed in black—cinematically conveying his evil heart—a fallen angel dares to approach God. Satan —which means adversary—is his name.

Unfazed, Father God simply asks, "What have you been up to?"

"A little of this and a little of that," Satan says, his eyes gleaming.

"What do you think about Job?" God asks. "He's the most righteous in all my creation."

"And why wouldn't he be?" Satan sneers. "You've blessed him without limit, and he enjoys an idyllic life. But take that away and watch him crumble."

"Very well," God answers. "I grant you authority to do as you wish. Just don't hurt him physically."

Satan nods. He leaves, rubbing his hands together in glee.

Doesn't this make for great drama? While theatrically pleasing, the scene is also theologically distressing.

Does Satan enjoy access to God's inner sanctum? The concept plays well in our movie. But knowing that God is present everywhere—omnipresent—the devil doesn't need to go to God. God exists wherever Satan happens to be.

And God doesn't need to ask what Satan's been doing. God knows all things—he's omniscient. He already knows what his adversary has done, but again, having God ask makes for good drama.

What's most troubling, however, is that God dangles the life of Job in front of Satan, baiting the devil to afflict Job. This thought doesn't comfort me. Even so, I must acknowledge God as sovereign, acting with absolute, supreme authority over his creation—of which Satan is a part.

I take solace in the fact that God is all-powerful—omnipotent. Whatever evil our enemy can concoct, God can overcome. He is also loving and compassionate. Don't forget this.

As we consider what Satan might do to Job, we can hold on to the reality of God's omnipotence, love, and compassion. This gives us hope that despite the turmoil of Job's story—and ours—we know that God will prevail and do what's best for us.

Do we cower in fear over what Satan can do to us or celebrate God's immense power that holds everything in his hands?

[Discover more about the awe-inspiring, amazing power of God in Nehemiah 9:6, Psalm 33:9, and Luke 1:37.]

DAY 3: SATAN'S ATTACK

JOB 1:13–19

"I am the only one who has escaped to tell you!" Job 1:15

With the opening scene of our movie establishing the setting for what is to come, we move on to scene two. It's on earth, not heaven. Job lounges inside his impressive home. It also functions as the headquarters of his domain. Recall that he's a powerful, respected, and wealthy man. He owns over 10,000 animals, with scores of hired hands overseeing his vast holdings.

The place bustles with activity, but Job relaxes amid it all. His staff's attention to details and their rush of movement surrounds his peaceful demeanor. He reclines as one of his servant girls feeds him grapes. Yes, it's cliché, but it helps show Job's situation for our movie's opening.

Shattering the peace, one of Job's most trusted servants rushes in. Panting, he shares alarming news. "We were attacked! Bandits stole all your oxen and donkeys. And in a bloody battle, they killed all the men. Only I escaped."

Staggering in behind the first servant shuffles another man, his singed clothes smoldering. He rubs his blackened face and wipes his watery eyes. "It began as a normal day," he pants. "Then fire shot down from heaven like lightning. It fried all your sheep in a flash and your shepherds too. Only I survived." Then the man crumples to the ground with a thud.

Before Job can react, a third man hobbles in, a gash across his face and blood dripping from his side. "They raided us! A coordinated attack. Three directions at once. They swooped in and drove off all your camels. We tried to stop them, but they were well armed, and we weren't. They slaughtered everyone, with only me barely escaping—"

"Your children!" screams a fourth man before the third one can finish. "Dead! All dead!" He gropes his tear-stained face. "Gale force winds.

They came from nowhere. Roaring like a tornado. The house collapsed, killing everyone inside, including all ten of your children. Of all your servants, only I survived."

In seconds, Job learns that his vast holdings are gone, swept away in one day. Even more distressing, his dear children are dead. He has nothing.

May we never face such severe devastation.

Knowing that our lives could change in an instant, where do we place our trust: possessions, family, or God?

[Discover more about another devastating situation in 1 Samuel 30:3–6.]

DAY 4: JOB'S RESPONSE
JOB 1:20–22

He fell to the ground in worship. Job 1:20

With Job receiving devastating news—times four—our camera zooms in for a close-up of his face. We watch his features twitch and then contort as the full impact of these demoralizing communiqués permeates the crevices of his consciousness. With a grimace, water wells up in his eyes.

"Gone. All gone," he moans. His shoulders droop. "Dead. All dead." He throws back his head and lets out a plaintive wail that echoes up to the heavens. His loud lament reverberates as his body quakes.

Fully spent, he struggles to his feet and grabs the lapels of his tunic. He pulls on them, trying to tear them. But he cannot rend the well-made garment. He relaxes his grasp and then slowly inhales, filling his lungs with strength for one all-out effort to rip his robe. This time he succeeds. He shreds the clothes that cover his body to reflect his torn soul inside.

He gets up and shaves his head—the proper appearance for a grieving heart. With each stroke of the blade he removes a bit more of the hair that proudly covered his once-regal crown. Tears stream down his face as he mindlessly completes his display of mourning.

With the second aspect of his outward posture of sorrow complete, he bows before God. But his effort at homage to the Almighty falters. Instead of bowing, he collapses to the ground in utter desolation. From a crumpled heap, he does the unexpected. He worships his creator.

"Just as I entered this world naked, so I will depart. I can take nothing with me." He opens his mouth to say more, but no words sound. On his third try, in a whisper he declares. "The good Lord gives, and the good Lord takes. Blessed be the name of the Lord."

The scene slowly fades to black, symbolically showing the end of the day along with the end of life as Job knows it.

Job has just received more devastation in a few minutes than most of us will receive in a lifetime. Despite this, we see no bitterness in his sorrow. He does not blame God for these tragedies. Instead, he acknowledges God's sovereignty and praises his character.

When troubles assault us, do we praise God or blame him?

[Discover more about other people who sought God from a place of deep despair in Joshua 7:6, 2 Samuel 13:19, 2 Kings 2:12, Esther 4:1, and Daniel 9:3.]

DAY 5: GOD AND SATAN, PART 2
JOB 2:1–6

"He is in your hands; but you must spare his life." Job 2:6

With the sun having set—both literally and figuratively—on the faithful Job, the next scene of our movie returns to God's palatial palace in the supernatural realm. Some time has passed since Satan afflicted the innocent Job. As the days tick by and the weeks unfold, Job stays steadfast in his devotion to God. Having watched his scheme against Job fail, Satan moves to phase two. This time he will succeed. This time he must.

Once again, just like every day, the angels make

their way to their creator's magnificent throne. They come to first worship and then to receive their assignments for the day. Their eyes twinkle in anticipation as they approach God's lofty perch to venerate their Lord. In turn, each receives his appointed task for the day, then hurriedly flies away to begin his work at once.

But the enemy is back in their midst. Standing in line with God's holy angel army is the unholy detestable devil. His black attire—now even more sinister-looking and fear-producing than before—stands as a harsh reminder of his foul character and his malevolent ploys.

Unfazed by Satan's return, Father God asks with unconcerned simplicity, "What have you been up to?"

"A little of this and a little of that," Satan again says with evasive disregard. Even so, his eyes are set with determination that this time his scheme will not fail.

"Have you considered Job's response to your unwarranted attack?" God asks. "Just as I suspected, he has maintained his integrity and not wavered in his devotion to me."

"And why not?" Satan scoffs in response. "You

kept me from afflicting him with physical pain. Let me do that, and he will most certainly falter, cursing you instead of praising you."

"Very well," God answers. "I grant you authority to do as you wish. Just don't kill him."

This time Satan makes no attempt to hide his glee. He sneers in anticipation of what he has in store for the innocent Job. With a blur of flapping wings, he flies off in haste to put phase two into action.

It's hard to balance God's sovereignty—to do whatever he wants—with the idea that he loves us like a perfect father who gives good gifts to his children and wants the best for us. We relish the idea of an omnipotent Father God who blesses us abundantly, but we squirm at the thought that he can also withdraw those same blessings.

How should we understand God's character when it doesn't make sense or when he disappoints us?

[Discover more about God's character in Numbers 23:19, Psalm 18:30, Psalm 116:5, Matthew 6:26, John 3:16–17, 1 Corinthians 10:13, James 1:17, 2 Peter 3:9, and 1 John 1:5.]

DAY 6: SATAN'S SECOND SALVO
JOB 2:7

So Satan . . . afflicted Job with painful sores from the soles of his feet to the crown of his head. Job 2:7

O ur next shot is from Satan's point of view. He spots Job from above and adjusts his trajectory, heading straight toward the now-pitiful man. Though we can see Satan's dive-bomb approach to Job through the camera's eye, Job cannot. And though we can hear the strained movement of Satan's wings as he closes in on his prey, Job cannot. Job can't see into the spiritual realm, and therefore he does not spot his enemy.

Job sits alone outside, perched next to a heap of

ashes. Cupping his hands, he scoops up a pile of the gray residue and throws it into the air. Much of it lands on his head and shoulders. Job repeats the process until he feels sufficiently covered with ash. His posture of mourning now complete—torn clothes, shaved head, and covered with ashes—he's left to ponder his situation and the focus of his devotion.

Satan beams with satisfaction at the desolate state of his subject. It will take little to push the sad and suffering man over the edge, driving him to renounce his faith and curse God. It shouldn't take long at all. The devil snickers, rubbing his hands together in glee—another movie cliché, but one that reveals our enemy's sinister character.

Oblivious to Satan's presence and unaware of the assault that's about to take place, Job stares into oblivion. All that once mattered to him is gone. He no longer has any reason to live.

Due to the authority God gave Satan to harass Job, the devil could afflict Job in the blink of an eye, but for the sake of our movie we'll invoke a bit of theatrics. Satan lands, stands tall, and stretches out his arms on each side. He whispers an incantation, one that sounds wicked even though we can't make out the words. He repeats the phrase over and over as it builds into a thunderous chant. In the spiritual realm, lightning flashes and thunder booms. But Job is unaware.

Satan thrusts his right arm into the air with his index finger extended. Giving a final shout, he drops his arm and plunges it straight toward Job. A flash of light emanates from Satan's pointed finger. In an instant, boil-like infections cover Job's whole body, from the bottom of his bare feet to the top of his ash-covered head.

Job recoils in pain and screams in agony. This time it's physical. He stares at his mottled skin and pus-filled sores. Just when he thought it couldn't get any worse, it does.

How might the knowledge that things could always be worse help us navigate life's difficulties?

[Discover more about an even greater agony in Luke 16:19–24.]

DAY 7: JOB'S REACTION
JOB 2:8–10

"Shall we accept good from God, and not trouble?" Job 2:10

Job finds a broken piece of pottery in the ashes. With a fatalistic sigh, he fishes out the shard and scrapes at his sores. It's a vain attempt to satiate the itch and remove the infected pus. Though it doesn't help much, doing something is better than doing nothing.

Job's wife strolls up. Her posture is not one of mourning but of contempt. Her face conveys no empathy. She offers no support. Instead, her words inflict even more pain on the suffering Job. "Look where your integrity has gotten you," she says. "Just curse God and die."

Job stares at her in disbelief. He hoped for comfort but received only opposition. "You don't get it. What right do we have to accept God's goodness and not hardship?"

She shakes her head and walks away.

It's easy to love God and worship him when things go well. When our lives are great and we receive his blessings, we can thank him, praise him, and appreciate his goodness.

However, life isn't always good. Sometimes our lives are a mess. When we don't receive God's blessings or experience his favor, do we still love him? We should, but our situation makes it a challenge. Hardship turns some people's appreciation of God into blame. Although understandable, this isn't right.

When we adore God during the good times, we may worship him because of what he's done for us. We adore him for his favor. We affirm him for his blessings. We praise him because he's benevolent.

But when we face difficulties, we must love him too. This is much harder, but we must press forward to appreciate God, despite our circumstances. He deserves our devotion regardless of our situation.

At first Job has every reason to love God because of what God did for him. And when it's all taken away Job has an understandable reason to turn from God and blame him. But Job doesn't.

Job's wife condemns him for maintaining his affirmation of God, his love for his creator. But despite all Job is going through, he doesn't blame God. And he doesn't sin.

The way we show God we appreciate him may vary with our circumstances; however, we should always love him. It's easy to adore God because of what he does for us, but we must also affirm him despite whatever hardships we're going through.

How can we best encourage someone when they suffer? How can we support them when circumstances challenge their faith?

[Discover more about another woman's reactions to her husband in 1 Samuel 19:11–12 and 2 Samuel 6:16–23.]

DAY 8: JOB'S FRIENDS
JOB 2:11–13

No one said a word to him, because they saw how great his suffering was. Job 2:13

As we continue our movie, Job's unsupportive wife walks away, and our camera focuses on his sorrow-filled face. As his facial features tremble and then contort, we're left wondering how much more Job can endure—and for how long. Remaining on the shot long enough to make us squirm, the camera then pulls back, way back. Soon Job is a mere dot on the horizon.

In the foreground, a camel ambles into view. The animal, adorned with showy accessories, suggests it carries nobility. As the camel plods forward, the first glimpse of its rider confirms our suspicions. The man—donned in a royal turban, dripping with jewels, and a purple robe of exquisite construction—glides forward with shoulders back and head held high. Regal to the max.

He halts his camel at the top of the hill. Using his hand as a visor to shield his eyes from the sun's glare, he gazes toward Job. The rider's shoulders sag. A second camel arrives with a rider as impressive as the first. Then a third animal and stately rider join them. The sight of pitiful Job in the distance appalls all three. They glance at each other wordlessly, but their eyes speak volumes.

A fourth man—younger and not as impressively attired—arrives on his camel. He pauses next to his three older friends. His face grows grim. At last the first man gives a subtle downward dip of his head and clicks his tongue. His camel lurches forward, and the other three follow.

Our camera zooms in again on Job. When he spots his friends approaching, his countenance brightens a bit. We dissolve into a scene of the four sitting with Job. They form a circle around the heap of ashes that is now the center of Job's reality.

The faces of the four men convey shock and

disbelief. No one says a word. They can't. The sun goes down on their silence. Fade to black.

The Bible says the men sat in silence for seven days and seven nights. We don't know if this is literal or hyperbole to make a point, but we do realize they stay quiet for a long time.

Sometimes we say more through our silence than our words.

How can we best help someone who is suffering? Can we discern when silence will provide them with the best support?

[Discover more about suffering in Acts 5:41, Romans 5:3–5, Romans 8:17–18, 2 Corinthians 1:6–7, and Colossians 1:24.]

DAY 9: JOB'S DEEPEST FEARS

JOB 3

"What I feared has come upon me; what I dreaded has happened to me." Job 3:25

Dawn arrives. We see Job and his four friends where we left them: sitting in a circle around the heap of ashes. The four men haven't said a word to their grieving friend. They seem content to let him speak first. They wait. And they wait some more.

Job inhales, filling his lungs in preparation to speak. He opens his mouth and air escapes, but his intended words fall short with an inhuman croak. He tries a second time without success. He scoops up a handful of ashes and throws it over himself.

The gray residue sticks to the moistness on his cheeks. He tips his head back and howls heavenward. With another intake of breath, he wills himself to speak.

"Oh . . . " But he can't finish. He tries again.

"Oh, that . . ." He closes his eyes and his head falls forward. With a shudder he pulls in a slow draught of air.

"Oh, that I had never been born." These are his first words since he rebuked his wife for her unhelpful advice.

The friends glance at each other but hold their thoughts private. They return their gaze to Job.

Emboldened by his success in finally saying a complete sentence, his confidence to speak builds. "I curse the day of my birth. Better that I died then, with my body cast aside, instead of a life reduced to this pitiful, meaningless existence. I wish I had never even been conceived."

His friends do nothing but stare.

Job continues. "My life now consists of sighs and groans—nothing more. It's all I have left." He looks up and locks eyes with the first man. "What I feared most in life has happened. Gone. All gone. Everything gone. My children have all died. Dead. All dead. I have nothing left. No reason to live."

Though God deserves our praise, sometimes we don't feel like it. Assuming we're honest about it, that's okay. I suspect God prefers to hear our honest angst over heaping him with insincere worship.

As Job winds down his soul-rending lament, he reveals the root of his despair: The thing he feared most, happened. He lost his wealth and his family.

Our enemy, Satan, realizes what each one of us fears most. It's not that he knows everything like God, but he is a great observer of what we say and do. He realizes what we're afraid of. Every chance he gets, he will use it against us to torment us and afflict us.

Although it's hard to shove aside our deepest fears and hide them from our enemy, we can turn them over to God. Once we do this, we can trust him to carry our fears and protect us from the onslaught of the enemy's attacks.

What are our deepest fears? Are we willing to turn them over to God and trust him with the outcome?

[Discover more about sharing our angst with God in Psalm 5 and Psalm 102.]

DIG DEEPER: WHAT'S A LEVIATHAN?

Leviathan the coiling serpent; he will slay the monster of the sea. Isaiah 27:1

The Bible refers to an animal called Leviathan. We don't know what kind of creature it is, but it shows up six times in Scripture: three times in Job, twice in Psalms, and once in Isaiah.

From these six accounts, we can piece together some ideas about Leviathan. It's a sea creature of terrifying presence. One passage talks of its limbs, strength, and grace. Isaiah calls it a serpent.

There are three thoughts about a leviathan.

One is that it is a mythological creature that never existed. It stands for an evil force, possibly Satan.

The second understanding is that a leviathan is an ancestor of today's crocodile.

A third view is that a leviathan was a real animal that is now extinct. But don't think that it died during the great deluge. All six of the Bible's leviathan mentions occur in books written *after* Noah and the flood.

We'll never know for sure.

What a leviathan was and represents remains for us to ponder. It's one more mystery of God that we can contemplate. This—and all of God's other mysteries—will one day become clear.

How can our understanding of leviathan help us on our faith journey?

[Discover more about Leviathan in Job 3:8, Job 41:1, Job 41:12, Psalm 74:13–14, and Psalm 104:26.]

DAY 10: ELIPHAZ SPEAKS
JOB 4–5

"Blessed is the one whom God corrects; so do not despise the discipline of the Almighty." Job 5:17

The first of Job's friends to make a noise, Eliphaz, clears his throat. Everyone looks at him. With a bit of theatrics, he stands, elevating himself to a position that commands their attention. With all eyes upon him, he stares down at Job.

Eliphaz begins his discourse. "At last I feel free to speak. Just as you have given advice to many over the years—to instruct them, strengthen them, and support them—I now address you. Be patient for a moment as I enlighten you.

"You are fickle, Job. At the first sign of trouble you grow discouraged. When calamity strikes, you become dismayed. Shouldn't you place your confidence and hope in your life of supposed right living?

"Consider, has God ever harmed the innocent? Has he afflicted the righteous? Of course not! Everyone reaps what they sow. And what you sowed has now revealed your true character. Don't play innocent with me. I'm on to you.

"Who are you to question God? Do you think you're better than him? If he judges angels for their sins, he'll surely judge you for yours. So then, appeal to God and confess your errors. May he offer you mercy, even though you don't deserve it.

"Job, you will do well to receive God's correction as a blessing. Don't dismiss his discipline. Though he afflicts you with pain now, he can later heal you—if only you will listen to my words and receive the lesson God is trying to teach you.

"You know I speak what is true. Carefully consider what I've just said, and apply it to your situation."

Eliphaz gives a decisive downward tip of his head to show that he has finished speaking. Then he sits.

Eliphaz has had a long time to consider what he will say to Job. Though his words could have offered comfort to his suffering friend, instead they come out as an accusation, judging Job for presumed shortcomings.

Eliphaz doesn't know Job's heart, and he certainly lacks an understanding of God's perspective, but Eliphaz speaks as though he knows both. In truth, his words may be more directed to himself than to Job.

We would do well to not make the same mistake.

How can we make sure our words help people and don't cause pain? When we share insights with others, are we trying to serve them or are we speaking to ourselves?

[Discover more about God's discipline in Deuteronomy 8:5, Proverbs 3:11–12, Jeremiah 10:24, 1 Corinthians 11:32, Hebrews 12:7–11, and Revelation 3:19.]

DAY 11: JOB RESPONDS TO ELIPHAZ
JOB 6–7

"Teach me, and I will be quiet; show me where I have been wrong." Job 6:24

As Job's countenance falls and his shoulders drop, he watches Eliphaz sit. Job lets out a slow, painful breath. He clamps his jaw and blinks to hold back the flood of tears that threatens to gush forth. He glances at the three other men, hopeful that they will come to his defense. Instead of speaking up for him, each one, in turn, averts his gaze.

Job redirects his attention to Eliphaz. "The burden of my misery is more than I can bear. There is no scale large enough to weigh it. The Lord has attacked me, zapping me of what little strength I have left.

"If only God would crush me for good and put an end to my pain. I have no reason to hope. My prospects are nil. There is no point in pursuing this patience you speak of. Things will never get better. I have no chance to turn my life around.

"Why do you withhold kindness from me, my so-called friend? You could have been God's instrument to encourage me, but you fail to do his bidding. You're undependable and no help. Your words mean nothing.

"Yes, I'm listening and am ready to learn. If only you would say something worthwhile. If only you could prove to me what I've done wrong. But as it is, you're full of hot air. You can't even look at me with kindness. I beg you to treat me fairly. To reconsider your attacks on my integrity. What have I done wrong for you to treat me so badly?

"Life is meaningless. I can't sleep at night and don't want to get up in the morning. My festering frame is all I have left. Sores spread across every inch of my skin. Worms scuttle over my body. I have every right to complain. My spirit is in anguish. My soul oozes bitterness.

"Tell me, how have I sinned? What do you have

against me? Why do you attack me without reason? I've given up and will soon die. Then it will be too late for you to help."

Job's response to Eliphaz reveals his deep despair. In viewing Job's situation, we can understand his depressed attitude. He hoped for compassion from Eliphaz, but he received only criticism. Job truly needs a friend, but his friend let him down.

Have we ever felt like Job? Have we ever had a friend who talked like him? What did we do?

[Discover more about despair and discouragement in Psalm 4:1, Psalm 6:2–3, Psalm 13:1–2, Psalm 22:1–2, and many other Psalms.]

DAY 12: BILDAD SPEAKS
JOB 8

"If you are pure and upright, even now he will rouse himself on your behalf and restore you to your prosperous state." Job 8:6

Hoping to dismiss the critical words of his first friend, Eliphaz, Job fixes his gaze on the second man, Bildad. Job dares not to try to speak, for his words will certainly fail him. But his eyes beg Bildad for help.

Bildad sneaks a sideways glance at Eliphaz who, with a quick dip of his head, grants Bildad permission to speak.

Bildad follows the example of his slightly older friend and stands to offer his wisdom. He puffs out his chest and grabs the lapels of his emerald-green robe. The sun glitters off his matching, jewel-encrusted turban. With a dramatic intake of breath, Bildad launches into his discourse, his eyes fixed on Job, as if drilling into the depths of his soul.

"How long, Job, will you persist in your perverse thinking? As it is, your words bluster like the wind. Consider the Lord God Almighty. Does he ever promote injustice? May it never be! Does he ever twist what is proper, what is right? Of course not! When sin occurs, he punishes it. Sit with that thought for a bit, Job—if you dare.

"If you seek him, if you plead for mercy, and if you are truly pure, then he will surely restore all you've lost. It starts with humility—something you sorely lack—but you can't even do that.

"If you are truly without blame, he will not reject you. He will fill you with joy. The fact that he hasn't done so proves that you're at fault, that you deserve what you've received, and that he will never rescue you. You brought this all upon yourself, my friend."

Bildad looks at Job's situation and assumes he deserves what he has received. Bildad equates right living with God's favor and hardship with sin and God's displeasure. While this certainly can be the case, it isn't an absolute rule. This reality is hard for many people to accept. It doesn't seem fair.

Remember, however, that God is sovereign, and in our limited understanding we may fail to see his perspective. That's why it sometimes seems that good things happen to bad people and bad things happen to good people.

Yet, God has a master plan, and we must trust him with that plan.

How do we react to the thought that God is sovereign? What can we do to better align our perspective with his?

[Discover more about God's plan for us in Jeremiah 29:11, Romans 5:8, and Romans 8:28.]

DAY 13: JOB RESPONDS TO BILDAD
JOB 9–10

"If only there were someone to mediate between us, someone to bring us together, someone to remove God's rod from me, so that his terror would frighten me no more." Job 9:33–34

As Bildad sits, a pleased smirk playing on his lips, Job shakes his head and lowers his gaze, fixated on the heap of ashes before him. Bildad's words, too, fell short of the comfort that Job hoped his long-time friend would give. Instead, Bildad's monologue stirred frustration in Job's mind. Without looking up, Job speaks.

"I get what you're saying and agree with it to some extent. But how can I, a mortal man whom God created, prove my innocence to him? He's

God. I'm nobody. He's wise and powerful, controlling his creation with no effort. Who am I to him? I'm nothing. I can't defend myself, debate his decisions, or argue against his wisdom.

"I've done nothing wrong, but he doesn't care. Whether good or bad, we will all die. May my end come soon. If only there were someone to represent me to him, someone who could reconcile us and remove his punishment.

"I hate my life. I plead with the Almighty to give me a not guilty verdict. At least tell me what I've done wrong. As it is, he seems to delight in tormenting me, even though I'm innocent.

"He created me, so I suppose he can do whatever he wants. But does it make sense for him to destroy what he has made? I think not. If only I had died at birth, but here I am. As my life approaches its end, will he relent in his affliction of me—for but a moment—so that I may have one last taste of joy before I die?"

Though Bildad has provided Job with something to think about, it does nothing to ease Job's disquiet. Though Job maintains his innocence, he feels that God has punished him anyway, as though he's guilty. But who is Job to contend with God, to present his case so that he can vindicate himself?

We understand God as approachable. We know he wants us to live in community with him, but Job doesn't see this. Perhaps he can't.

Remember that Job wishes someone could come to mediate between him and God, someone who could bring them together, someone to remove God's punishment and take away Job's fear.

Jesus is that mediator for us. He gave his life for us to reconcile us with Papa, removing our punishment for our wrongdoing and taking away any fear we may have.

Do we see Jesus as our mediator? Have we accepted his work so that we may live in community with him?

[Discover more about Jesus as our mediator and Savior in John 14:6, Romans 8:38–39, Hebrews 9:15, and 1 Timothy 2:5.]

DIG DEEPER: THE ALLURE OF MYSTERY

"Can you fathom the mysteries of God?" Job 11:7

There are things about God, Jesus, and salvation that the Bible simply describes as *mystery*. It's a hidden truth or a mystic secret that is beyond our comprehension.

This drives some people crazy.

It confronts their faith in God. They want to understand all and be able to fully explain everything. Anything less riles up frustration. It generates a spiritual angst.

However, the realization that some things of God are but a mystery draws others to him. It is an allure. Daily we strive to unravel this mystery and know him more fully, all the while realizing we'll never completely achieve our goal. This is as it should be.

God and his ways are a mystery. Mystery entices us to pursue him. Mystery serves as an attraction, which draws us to him.

May we embrace the mystery of God and his ways.

How willing are we to accept that some things about God are a mystery? Does this produce comfort or cause consternation?

[Discover more about the mystery of God in Romans 11:25–26, 1 Corinthians 15:51–52, Ephesians 3:6, Ephesians 5:32, Ephesians 6:19, Colossians 2:2, Colossians 4:3, 1 Timothy 3:16, and Revelation 10:7.]

DAY 14: ZOPHAR SPEAKS
JOB 11

"Yet if you devote your heart to him and stretch out your hands to him . . . then . . . you will stand firm and without fear." Job 11:13, 15

The two older men, Eliphaz and Bildad, have had their say. Now all eyes turn to the third of Job's friends, Zophar. Realizing that at last he will have a chance to speak, the corners of his mouth turn up a bit to reveal the hint of a smile. Zophar is a rotund man and shorter than his two peers. Though a couple years younger, his added heft makes him look older. He doesn't bother to stand. It will take too much effort. He is the most sloppily dressed among the group, but the multiple gold chains hanging around his neck and jeweled rings on his fingers confirm he's a man of great wealth, albeit messy in appearance.

He clears his throat, first because he needs to and a second time because he wants to. Having secured everyone's attention, he pauses to heighten the anticipation for the wisdom he's about to share. With time to corral his thoughts and carefully plan his words, he wants to make sure everyone hears what he has to say.

"Do you think, Job, that your many words will exonerate you? Do you expect your lengthy comeback to lull us into silence? Will no one rebuke you? Well, I will!

"You claim to be sinless and pure. You think you're innocent. Oh, that God would share his thoughts with us. But know this: he will never forget your sins.

"Who are you to contend with the Almighty? He's the creator and you are his creation. Those he convicts have no rebuttal. Those he throws in jail have no expectation of parole. He knows who is for him and who is against him.

"The situation is obvious. If you devote yourself

to him, worship him, and stay far from sin, then he will bless you. He will elevate you and declare you faultless. Then you can stand before him in confidence and without fear. You will experience his favor. But as for the wicked, they will fail, they will not escape, and their only hope is death."

Like his two friends before him, Zophar does nothing to offer Job comfort or clarity. Instead, Zophar uses the logic of an incomplete theology to conclude that Job is suffering so much because he has sinned.

In his monologue, Zophar says that Job thinks his beliefs are flawless. Ironically, Zophar acts the same way about his. Many people carry this assumption that their beliefs are without error. Yes, we must seek truth in our pursuit of God, but we must hold it loosely. After all, we may be wrong.

Therefore, we should adopt the humble viewpoint that our beliefs *may* be flawed. Remember, God and faith are mysteries. Later, we will see in full, but for now our view of God is incomplete.

How tightly do we hold on to our beliefs? Our theology? How open are we to accept someone whose views are contrary to ours?

[Discover more about grasping spiritual truth in 1 Corinthians 13:12.]

DAY 15: JOB RESPONDS TO ZOPHAR
JOB 12–14

"You will call and I will answer you; you will long for the creature your hands have made." Job 14:15

When Zophar ends his monologue, he raises his eyebrows to highlight the smug satisfaction he holds for his words. Eliphaz and Bildad nod their approval. However, Job doesn't share their perspective. Zophar, like his two friends, did not console Job or give him any useful feedback. Instead, Zophar heaped more pain on Job.

For his part, Job shakes his head and returns his focus to the ash heap before him. Though the pile of residue doesn't offer any words of comfort, at least it doesn't throw words of condemnation in his face. He stares at the grayscale cinders as he contemplates what to say. He draws in deep reserves of air several times before opening his mouth to speak.

"Oh, you are so wise! Surely when you die, you will take all wisdom with you. But I'm a person just like you. Your thoughts are no better than mine. So why, my friends, do you laugh at my fate?

"God is wise. He holds all power. He under-stands everything. What he says goes, punishing those he wishes to punish. We both know this. My situation does not make me any less than you.

"You lie to me—all three of you. What a bunch of worthless consolers. You'd accomplish more if you'd just keep quiet. Not saying a word would be the wisest thing you can do.

"Though God seems distant, I'll place my hope in him. I'll defend myself to his face. I trust he will deliver me from my afflictions. That I'll receive vindication in the end.

"Yes, I'm discouraged with all of life's troubles, of its brevity and pain, but when he calls me, I will answer. Surely, he will cover my sin."

The critical response of Job's friends doesn't supply the comfort Job needs, and God's distance confuses him. Yet Job remains steadfast in his confidence in God, and his faith doesn't waver.

Do we expect God to call to us? How do we respond when he does? What about when he seems silent?

[Discover more about God calling us in John 10:3 and 1 Thessalonians 5:24.]

DIG DEEPER: HOPE

"Though he slay me, yet will I hope in him; I will surely defend my ways to his face." Job 13:15

The word hope appears ninety-seven times in the Old Testament, in sixteen of the thirty-nine books. Interestingly, *hope* doesn't show up in the first seven books of the Bible. Psalms overflows with *hope*, thirty-four times. The book of Job comes in second with eighteen mentions. The Old Testament prophets also mention *hope*. They look forward in hopeful expectation to a better future.

Some people follow Jesus for the hope he gives them for a better tomorrow in this life. That's a start. Other people pursue Jesus for the hope he gives them for a better tomorrow in the afterlife. And that's another reward.

The Bible overflows with hope, and as we study it, we should overflow with it ourselves: hope for tomorrow and hope for beyond.

How well do we do in placing our hope in God? Do the Bible's passages on hope encourage us for what is to come?

[Discover more about hope in Psalm 37:9, Isaiah 40:31, Romans 5:2, Colossians 1:5, and 1 Peter 1:13.]

DAY 16: ELIPHAZ DOUBLES DOWN
JOB 15

"Listen to me and I will explain to you." Job 15:17

After Job has vented his frustration in response to the accusatory words of Zophar, he leans forward and cradles his head in his hands. His shoulders quake as he tries to corral his surge of emotions. He sits in silence, giving time for his angst to abate.

His mind flashes back to an earlier time, a happier time—and our movie takes us there. The setting is Job's home, and the scene is of his ten young children sitting around him. They play and laugh and sing. Smiles abound, especially for Job and even for his wife. It's a time when life is good.

Idyllic. Perfect even. The thought of what once was brings a momentary sense of joy to Job. But it's fleeting because when Job glances up, Eliphaz again opens his mouth.

"Would a man who is truly wise talk as you do? Your speeches rage like a hot wind, full of useless thoughts and misconceived ideas. Sin drives your words, and through them you condemn yourself.

"Who do you think you are? How dare you act like you're smarter than us, that you alone hold wisdom. Aren't God's words enough for you? Even so you rage against him.

"If you listen to me, I will explain this truth to you. Look at me Job. Hear my words and understand what is real. Men are wicked, and you're just like them. That's why you're so distressed and full of anguish, with hardship overwhelming you. That explains why God stripped your wealth from you. You will not escape punishment. You will die before your time because you pursue evil."

Eliphaz persists in the notion that the hardship Job endured stands as a confirmation of Job's evil heart and a mark of God's disapproval. In Eliphaz's condescending attitude he tries to instruct Job.

But Eliphaz speaks through arrogance and ignorance. His view of God is incomplete—just as ours is—so his conclusions are deficient. And when he casts his flawed logic on Job, he inflicts unnecessary pain on his friend.

We should be careful that our efforts to teach others do no harm. Furthermore, we must take care not to judge others through the lens of our own incomplete theology. We should leave judgment to God.

When has the way we've shared our view of God (our theology) hurt others? How can we accept people without judging them?

[Discover more about instructing others in Proverbs 1:8, Proverbs 22:6, Titus 2:1–10, and James 3:1. Learn more about judging others in Luke 6:37, 1 Corinthians 4:4, and James 2:3–4.]

DAY 17: JOB MAINTAINS HIS INNOCENCE

JOB 16–17

"But my mouth would encourage you; comfort from my lips would bring you relief." Job 16:5

J ob locks eyes with Eliphaz, a man he once considered his friend. When Eliphaz spoke a second time, he had an opportunity to correct the hurtful words he said earlier, to offer Job the comfort he longs to hear. Eliphaz did not, and Job vents in frustration.

"You three have done such a pitiful job consoling me. You drone on and on with your diatribes against me. Will you never tire of your worthless lectures? There must be something wrong with you to persist with the things you say.

"If our roles were reversed, I could give clever speeches and look down upon you. But I would not. I would speak words of encouragement. I would give you messages of comfort, showering you with support.

"Talking about my situation does not alleviate my pain. But keeping quiet doesn't help either. For whatever reason, God is against me. His attacks have left me devastated. I've replaced my torn robe with sackcloth. I've covered myself with dust. My face is red, swollen from endless tears.

"Despite all that's happened, I've done no wrong. My prayers to the Almighty remain pure. God in heaven stands as my witness. He knows what is true. He serves as my advocate when I pray. As I cry out to him, he is my intercessor. Even so, I know I will soon die.

"I beg you all, try again to comfort me. Have you no wisdom to share? So far, you've failed. Death remains my only hope."

Job criticizes his friends for their failure to help him, to alleviate his pain. Though he says he could treat them the same way if they switched places, he would not. Instead he would speak words of reassurance. He would console them.

Based on what he says he will do, by implication he would not judge them, direct accusatory lectures at them, or insist that they had done wrong, thereby incurring God's wrath.

Job would extend them hope in a hopeless situation.

How can we better offer hope to hurting people? How can we help people when we speak?

[Discover more about helping people with our words in Proverbs 15:1, Ephesians 4:15, and 1 Peter 3:15–16.]

DIG DEEPER: SOMETIMES THE BEST THING TO SAY IS NOTHING

Make it your ambition to lead a quiet life: You should mind your own business. 1 Thessalonians 4:11

A recurring theme throughout the book of Job is that his friends' words are unhelpful and received as torment. When Job's visitors talk, their words only deepen his distress. They give pompous speeches as Job struggles with his tenuous grasp on his faith in God. His friends do not help him feel better.

Job grows exasperated with their failed attempts to offer support. He wishes they would keep quiet. He says that by saying nothing they would better display their wisdom. Though this might be a bit of hyperbole on Job's part, he offers wise advice.

Often words are inadequate. Sometimes speaking hurts more than it helps. Job doesn't need his friends to try to explain his situation, offer a theological response, or interject their own perspectives. They could have helped him more by simply being present and saying nothing.

Offering others our presence may be exactly what they need, but we can mess that up when we try to offer them our words too. Anyone can go and sit with a friend in need. The best friends know when to talk and when to be quiet. And the best gift is often the gift of silence.

Just ask Job.

Do we find it hard to sit in silence with a suffering friend? What does our mere presence say to those in pain?

[Discover more about how we use our words in Job 13:5, Job 16:2–3, and Job 19:2.]

DAY 18: BILDAD ATTACKS

JOB 18

"Be sensible, and then we can talk." Job 18:1

Job shifts his gaze from Eliphaz to Bildad, suspecting he will now speak again. With his jaw clamped tight, Job hopes for a reprieve from the second man, though not daring to expect anything different from his once-valued friend.

Bildad sighs and glares at Job. Without a hint of kindness in his eyes or compassion on his face, Bildad shakes his head with sadness and launches into a second diatribe.

"When, Job, will you cease your lengthy discourses? If only you would open your mind so you could truly listen, then we could have a meaningful conversation. But that won't happen until you stop being so defensive. We're not stupid like you think. Take a moment and try to hear the wisdom we have to share.

"The light of a wicked man grows dim. His home becomes dark. Though he once walked with vigor, he now shuffles forward, his own schemes dragging him down. Like a trap snapping at his foot or a snare entangling his body, he has no chance of escape. A noose awaits him.

"As his life spirals down, terrors torment him, and disaster dogs him with each step. His skin sloughs away, and his appendages atrophy. He's torn from his sanctuary, the place where he once felt secure. His possessions disappear until he has nothing left.

"People will soon forget him. He will leave no legacy. Without an heir, no one will remember him or mourn his passing. Such is the outcome for an evil man, of someone who does not know God."

Bildad ends his attack raising his eyebrows with superior condescension. He dips his head down as he glares at Job, confirming that these words apply directly to the suffering man.

Bildad assumes that he knows the truth and Job is in error, since his life is on track and Job's is not. Bildad acts as though his prosperity gives him the right to speak, and Job's destitution requires him to listen.

But a high status does not make us wise. Neither does a low position mean we're foolish. True wisdom comes from God and him alone, as guided by the Holy Spirit. Though Bildad thinks he has something worthwhile to say, he is wrong. His words shoot forth as arrows, inflicting hurt as well as failing to help.

What can we do to make sure the words we say build people up and not tear them down? Do we need to speak less and listen more?

[Discover more about controlling our words in Ephesians 4:29, James 1:19–20, and James 3:4–5.]

DAY 19: JOB AFFIRMS GOD
JOB 19

"I know that my redeemer lives." Job 19:25

After Bildad's attack, Job stares into the distance. He sits in silence as if this time he will not respond. Still, his anger bubbles within him, slowly at first and then building until it boils. He scans the three men and closes his eyes. He draws in a deep breath, filling his lungs as if for a final salvo.

"How long will you three persist in tormenting me? Why do you insist on continuing to pile your heavy words on my back? If I am in error, then it is my issue and none of your business.

"I cry out to God for help, but I receive no

justice. For some reason he opposes me and stays distant. He's taken away my honor. In his anger he treats me like an enemy, sending his army to surround me and place me under siege.

"What little family I have left, God has estranged them from me. Everyone I know has deserted me. Even my servant ignores me when I beg for his help. My wife won't even come near me. All I have left is this broken body.

"Why won't you take pity on me? God has struck me. Why do you too? Must you also add to my pain?

"Yes, I know that God exists. He'll vindicate me in the end. Soon I will die, and then I'll see him with my own eyes. Oh, how my soul longs for that to happen.

"But as for you three, don't worry about me. Worry about yourself and the judgment you will each face."

Job's friends attack him with their words. And Job believes that God opposes him for a reason he can't understand. The three men condemn Job out of their ignorance, and God seems to deny Job the justice he seeks. Despite all this, Job continues to trust God with his eternal destiny.

Though Job roils in physical anguish and emotional turmoil now, he still expects that God will redeem him. Job looks beyond the pain of his life to expect that when he dies, he will see God at last. And he can't wait for that encounter to take place.

When has our faith wavered? How can we keep our allegiance to God despite the circumstances of our life, whether deserved or undeserved?

[Discover more about keeping our focus on God in Deuteronomy 6:5, Matthew 6:31–33, Matthew 22:37, and Colossians 3:2.]

DIG DEEPER: SCRIPTURAL
REFERENCES TO JOB

*You have heard of Job's perseverance and have seen what the
Lord finally brought about.* James 5:11

I n addition to James mentioning Job in his letter (James 5:11), Ezekiel also refers to Job twice in his prophetic book (Ezekiel 14:14 and 14:20).

Beyond that, Paul quotes from the book of Job in his letters to the churches in Corinth and Rome. Interestingly, neither of these quotes come from sections which record God's spoken word.

Instead, the first comes from the lips of Eliphaz, while the second is from Job himself. Even though we have reason to question Eliphaz's overall theology, Paul implicitly affirms part of it by selecting this phrase to include in his letter to the Corinthians. We can draw the same conclusion with Job's words that Paul selects to share with the Romans.

- Job 5:13 is in 1 Corinthians 3:19.
- Job 41:11 is in Romans 11:35.

Overall, when we think of Job, we esteem a man who suffered innocently, persevered diligently, and received rewards abundantly.

How can we apply Job's example to our lives? How can Job inspire us to do better?

[Discover more about perseverance in Romans 5:3–4, Hebrews 12:1–2, James 1:2–4, and 2 Peter 1:5–7.]

DAY 20: ZOPHAR STRIKES AGAIN
JOB 20

"Such is the fate God allots the wicked, the heritage appointed for them by God." Job 20:29

Eliphaz and Bildad have both spoken to Job twice. Zophar will now take his second turn. With much effort, the plump man stands to address Job. By elevating himself when he speaks, he hopes Job will listen this time.

Zophar puffs out his chest and fingers the largest of his gold chains. On this one hangs a glittering medallion, no doubt signifying an honor he holds dear. By touching this pendant, he intends to communicate his high standing and the validity of what he is about to say. He hopes Job will pick up on this subtle hint.

"Where should I even begin? I came here to help you. I tried to speak truth to you, but you dare to attack me instead. Your mean-spirited words have caused me great distress. It compels me to defend my character to your troubling reproach.

"You know about God's ways from the beginning of time. Since the days of Adam, the Almighty has punished the wicked. Their life becomes but a flicker in time. Though in pride they stretch up to grasp the heavens, they still die. Everyone will forget them. The vigor of their youth will turn to dust as their bones decay.

"Though they once delighted in doing evil, it returns to them and causes their undoing. What they once did to the detriment of others will now come back on them. They will die for what they did.

"Their money will not save them. Their possessions offer no security. Even though their life may seem good for a season, it won't last. God will take them down. He'll reveal their sins for all to see. This is how God treats the wicked."

Zophar nods to Job, thereby applying the plight of the wicked to Job's unfortunate circumstances.

With a pleased smirk, Zophar winks at his two friends and then sits.

Zophar's theology is that God always punishes the wicked. He makes them suffer for what they've done. He concludes that since Job is undergoing great suffering, he must be wicked too.

Yes, Job is suffering. But we must remember that it's not for any fault he has committed. His wounds are not God's doing either. Job's pain comes from the adversary, Satan. We must be clear on this fact and not forget it.

How often do we wrongly blame God for what happens to us? How can we hold on to our faith when hardships shake us and cause our trust in him to falter?

[Discover more about trusting in God in Psalm 62:8, Proverbs 3:5, Matthew 6:25–34, and Philippians 4:6.]

DAY 21: JOB FIRES BACK

JOB 21

"Can anyone teach knowledge to God?" Job 21:22

Zophar's insistence that Job is suffering because he is wicked hits the hurting man hard. He isn't intent on doing evil, nor has he sinned.

Job scoops up another handful of ashes and dumps them on his boil-infested head. In deep distress, he moans. He picks up his shard of glass and resumes scraping the sores that cover his body. Though the relief lasts only a moment, his efforts give him time to formulate what he will say. At last he looks up and gives a blank stare to Zophar.

"If nothing else, will you at least listen to what I

have to say? Give me a chance to speak before you resume mocking me. I don't direct my complaint to you. My grievance is with God. Just take one look at my situation and you'll realize why I'm impatient.

"You say that God punishes evil, but from my perspective the wicked seem to live on. The older they get the more powerful they become. Their children flourish. Their homes stand strong as their refuge. As God's punishment delays, they continue to prosper. They feel self-sufficient and see no need to pursue God or to seek him in prayer.

"Who would dare to try to teach God anything? Remember, he stands above you and me. One person dies rich and satisfied, another ends poor and destitute. Even so they both go to the grave where worms feast off their decaying bodies.

"Why do you persist in spouting your poppycock? As it is, you offer me nothing but a mouthful of lies. Be quiet and leave me alone."

Zophar has spoken twice. Both times he accused Job of wrongdoing, of being wicked and doing what is evil. He justifies his conclusion with the simplistic logic that without fail God immediately curses the wicked and blesses the good. Therefore,

Job has most certainly done wrong, and God is punishing him for it.

To this argument, Job counters with his perspective that he sees the wicked flourish, with God delaying their punishment. By his own account, Job has already claimed that he suffers though innocent.

This is hard for us to understand. It strikes at our sense of what is fair. Who are we to understand God's ways? Who are we to teach him anything? Though we seem wise in our own eyes, our wisdom may appear as foolishness to him.

Do we think we are wise? Do we sometimes act like we know better than God?

[Discover more about what God thinks about wisdom and foolishness in 1 Corinthians 1:20, 25, and 27.]

DAY 22: ELIPHAZ TRIES AGAIN
JOB 22

"Is not your wickedness great? Are not your sins endless?"
Job 22:5

Job lets out a shallow breath, weak and barely discernible. He closes his eyes with care, as though it causes him pain. He pushes his mind to find that happier time with his children. The next scene of our movie takes us there. Job's mind, however, doesn't go to when his children were young and innocent. Instead, he sees them in a more recent time as adults, celebrating a festival at the oldest one's house.

Job is not present at their party, but he sees it through his imagination. They're dressed in their finest as they enjoy a great feast. They make merry amid a cornucopia of food and drink. They truly enjoy the presence of one another. His oldest son stands and gives a grand toast to their generous and loving father. They raise their glasses in agreement and clink them together in confirmation. "To father Job!" the oldest proclaims. Everyone agrees with a great hurrah and then takes a sip of wine.

Eliphaz clears his throat, jerking Job from his memories and returning him to his present pain. "Could even the best of us offer anything of value to God? If we behave would that please him? Think about your situation, Job. Has he attacked you because you are good and without sin? Of course not!

"You neglected to provide people in need with water, food, and clothes. You failed to give money to widows and orphans. These omissions have brought you to where you are now. God sees all. Those with evil hearts want nothing to do with him even though he gives them nice things. Even so, good people will celebrate the downfall of the wicked.

"My advice to you is to yield to the Almighty

and seek peace with him. Then he will bless you with good fortune. Do what he says and return to him. Then he will restore to you what he took away. In his goodness, he even rescues those who are not innocent."

Eliphaz views our relationship with God as transactional. He assumes that if we behave, God will reciprocate by blessing us. On the other hand, if we do what is wrong, God will respond by chastising us. From Eliphaz's perspective, he sees Job's condition as God's punishment. The logical conclusion—though incorrect—is that Job suffers because of his sins.

God, in his mercy, does not give us the punishment we deserve. And God, in his grace, gives us good things we cannot earn. He loves us unconditionally. We can't gain his love because he has already given it to us.

How do we try to earn God's favor? Do we rely on good works or faith for our salvation?

[Discover more about God's grace in Acts 15:11 and Ephesians 2:8–9. Learn more about God's mercy in Ephesians 2:4–5 and Titus 3:4–7.]

DAY 23: JOB DEFENDS HIMSELF
JOB 23–24

"My feet have closely followed his steps; I have kept to his way without turning aside." Job 23:11

Job scrunches his eyebrows and glares at Eliphaz.

"Why won't you listen to me? Do you still not understand? Though I groan to the Almighty, he does not respond. He is distant, and I cannot find him. If only I could see him face-to-face and make my defense. I'm sure he would hear me and consider my words, declaring me not guilty!

"But I cannot find him. I turn east and then west, but he is not there. I look north and south, but I don't see him. Still he knows me. He tested me, weighed me in his balance. As a result, I emerge as pure gold.

"My conscience is clear. With diligence I have followed him. With eyes looking straight ahead, I've stayed on the path he set for me. I've listened to his instructions and followed each one. The words from his mouth are more important to me than food."

Eliphaz fails to comfort Job. Instead, his arguments rile up anger. With a friend who speaks like Eliphaz, I'd be angry too. In Job's defense, he professes all he has done to align himself with God. He claims his practices prove his devotion to the Almighty.

First, Job says that he follows closely behind God. It's as if he walks in God's shadow, placing each step in the footprint of his Lord.

Next, Job keeps his eyes fixed on God, walking in his path. Job looks not to his left or to his right. He tunes out worldly distractions to remain aligned with God.

Third, Job obeys God's instructions. He listens to what God says and follows his directives with unswerving commitment.

Job ends his testimony asserting that he values God's words more than food. Though we might think this refers to the written Word of God, the Bible, it does not. Job likely lives in a time before the Scriptures existed, certainly before they were readily available. This means he treasures the *spoken* words of God. Job would rather feed his soul by listening to God than feed his body by eating food.

Job gives us an example of godly devotion we will do well to follow.

How devoted are we to following God? Will we continue to pursue him when we suffer and he seems distant?

[Discover more about following Jesus in Matthew 16:24, Luke 9:57–62, and John 10:3–6. Learn more about devotion to God in 2 Kings 20:3 and 1 Chronicles 28:9.]

DAY 24: BILDAD PROVIDES
SOMETHING TO CONSIDER
JOB 25

"How then can a mortal be righteous before God?"

Job 25:4

Just as Eliphaz has spoken three times, Bildad now takes his third turn. This time he doesn't bother to stand. Nor does he first glance at Eliphaz for approval to speak. Instead, Bildad looks at Job with a sad face and opens his mouth.

"God is in charge. Don't forget that. Who are we to understand him? We can't. His power is too great, his angels are too many, and his presence is everywhere.

"Can any of his mortal creation ever stand

before him as good enough? Of course not! We were born in sin, and our sinful nature compels us to do what is wrong. We'll never be pure enough to approach him on our own. To him we are but a maggot, a mere worm."

Bildad draws in a slow and shallow breath, closes his eyes, and lowers his head.

In the shortest of all the speeches, Bildad gives Job —and us—something to think about. Between worshiping God for who he is and acknowledging that we are nothing next to him, Bildad asks an unsettling question: "How can a mere mortal be worthy to stand before God?"

It's a rhetorical question. We can't. We aren't good enough, and we never will be.

In the Old Testament, God gave his people the Law through Moses. The Law was a complex set of rules for proper worship and right living. It was also impossible for anyone to fully follow. Does that mean everyone in the Old Testament died separated from God? No. Scripture tells us that Abraham, for example, was justified (accepted) because of his faith in God.

In the New Testament, we have Jesus. He fulfills

the Old Testament Law, offering himself as the ultimate sacrifice to end all sacrifices and thereby removing from our permanent record all the mistakes we've ever made or will make. This makes us right with God and able to stand before him.

There's nothing we can do to earn our salvation or make us right with God. It's a matter of faith. Our right standing with God is a gift he offers to everyone. All we need to do is accept it.

Though we can, and should, strive to change our behavior *after* we've been made right with God through faith, we do this as a thank you note for what he has done. It's a response, not a requirement. Doing good isn't a condition to achieve something he offers us as a gift—for free—with no strings attached.

How do we view our relationship with God? Are we trying to earn a gift he's already offered to us?

[Discover more about doing good works, faith, and salvation in Ephesians 2:8–9.]

DAY 25: WHO UNDERSTANDS GOD?

JOB 26

"Who then can understand the thunder of his power?" Job 26:14

After Bildad gives the shortest of all the speeches, Job responds with his longest one. Though his words initially spring from what Bildad just said, Job launches into a wide-ranging discourse where he recaps what he has already spoken, while adding new thoughts as well.

Though Bildad's eyes stay closed, Job looks his way anyhow. Next, he glances left to Zophar and then right to Eliphaz. No one acts as though they want to talk. The camera zooms in for a close-up of

Job, close enough to make us squirm at the intimate portrayal of this suffering man. Job's nostrils flare. He struggles to his feet. His aching bones make it hard to stand, but he eventually straightens his frame so that he's more or less erect. Beyond that, he doesn't try to command attention or perform any pre-speech rituals.

"Oh, great ones, you are too wise! Your words have helped me so much. Though I am weak, you rescued me. Compared to your vast knowledge I am nothing. Your insight flows forth without measure.

"Who gave you these words? Whose spirit inspired you?

"Consider the dead. They're . . . dead. They shudder in the grave because they are no more. But God knows all about them. He knows all details about all things.

"God controls the sky and the clouds, dispensing rain when he wills it. He governs the phases of the moon and separates light from darkness. Even heaven shakes at the sound of his thunderous reprimands. And this isn't even the half of it.

"Who then can comprehend all of this?"

Job affirms God's control over nature, over all his creation. If God can dictate what happens in space, the sky, and water, how much more can he do with us and for us?

We can't begin to fully understand him. Recall that God is a mystery, so not everything will make sense (Refer to "Dig Deeper: The Allure of Mystery").

One day we will know in full, but for now we can only begin to glimpse who he is and what he can do. It's like looking at our reflection in a lake or seeing our image in a dim mirror. For now, we can only gain a partial peek at what is. Later, the full picture will become clear.

How content are we to only understand God in part? How do we deal with the things we don't understand about him?

[Discover more about our ability to fully know God in Exodus 6:3, 1 Corinthians 13:12, and Ephesians 3:4–5.]

DAY 26: A CLEAR CONSCIENCE
JOB 27

"I will maintain my innocence and never let go of it." Job
27:6

J ob pauses to make sure the three men are listening. Then he continues his discourse.

"As sure as I stand before you, God withholds justice from me. His afflictions have ravaged my life and vexed my soul beyond comprehension.

"Despite all this, and though I have every reason to be bitter, for as long as I breathe, I won't utter a single evil thing. I will speak only truth and will refrain from lies. And I will never accept that you three know what you're talking about.

"Until I take my final breath, I will hold on to my integrity. I am innocent, innocent of all you charge me with. And I have a clear conscience that refuses to convict me of any wrongdoing.

"If you will but listen, it is *I* who will teach *you*. I will tell you about God and celebrate his immense power. I will not hold back what I know. I will reveal all that I understand. Then you will realize your words have no meaning.

"Yes, God does punish the wicked. But I am not one of them."

Though Job feels God denies him justice, he doesn't claim that God's behavior is unjust. This is key. Although it's okay to question God, we should never charge him with misconduct.

And though Job's body and soul writhe in anguish, he doesn't accuse God of wrongdoing. Yes, Job believes his afflictions come from God, but he stops short of blaming the Almighty for his misfortune.

Job perceives that God has punished him for an unknown reason. Add to this the accusations of the three men that Job is evil and guilty of wickedness. However, despite feeling that both God and the three men oppose him, Job commits to persisting in right behavior.

He will continue to do as he always has. He will not say anything wicked. Nor will he speak lies. Job will hold onto his veracity. He has a clear conscience in all things, not condemned of any wrongdoing.

Do we have a clear conscience before God and man? Will we persist in doing right despite enduring difficult circumstances or the hurtful words of others?

[Discover more about living life with a clear conscience in Acts 24:16, 2 Corinthians 1:12, and 1 Timothy 3:9.]

DAY 27: WISDOM
JOB 28

"But where can wisdom be found?" Job 28:12

Some versions of the Bible treat Job chapter 28 as an interlude, a parenthetical aside to teach about wisdom. Other versions show this chapter as a continuation of Job's lengthy discourse. In the case of our movie, we'll treat it as a voiceover, with words of insight coming from our narrator. Either way, we can consider the content of this chapter to glean insight from it.

Whether from Job's mouth or not, the words continue.

"People mine for silver and gold. When they find it, they purify it to produce something of value.

They dig into the earth for iron and copper, smelting it to produce ore that they can fashion into useful tools. They seek gems among the rocks. Though birds cannot see these reserves from the air, and animals do not perceive them from the ground, people pursue these treasures with great diligence.

"How much more should we search for wisdom, to amass understanding? Yet where can we find true knowledge? These are priceless finds. We cannot buy wisdom with gold or silver. We cannot trade precious stones to buy understanding.

"What is the source of wisdom? Where does it abide? Where does understanding live? How can we make our way to find it? Birds cannot see it, and animals cannot perceive it.

"God—and God alone—can explain the path to wisdom. Only he knows where it lives. Don't forget that he controls all of nature, so revealing true knowledge to us is a simple feat. At creation, God saw wisdom. He evaluated it, verified it, and tested it.

"Having done all this, he reveals his findings: 'Wisdom starts with fearing God,' he says. 'And the basis of understanding is to shun evil.'"

We place value on gold, silver, and jewels. We pursue and buy them. Still these tangible items are nothing compared to the intangible value of wisdom and understanding. As such, we should pursue these higher quests with more diligence. Material wealth means little compared to the immaterial.

We should seek what matters. We do this by fearing God and shunning evil.

What does it mean to fear God? Do we have true wisdom and understanding?

[Discover more about the source of wisdom in Psalm 90:12, Psalm 111:10, Proverbs 2:6, and James 1:5. In contrast, consider Genesis 3:6.]

DAY 28: HELP OTHERS
JOB 29

"I was like one who comforts mourners." Job 29:25

After Job gives his sarcastic retort followed by his serious rebuttal, he pauses for a moment to collect his thoughts. Then he continues sharing the agony of his heart.

"Oh, how I wish life could return to how it once was, when the Almighty watched over me and blessed me. Those were the good old days. Now they're gone. I was in my prime then. My children surrounded me and filled me with joy. Prosperity abounded.

"Back then, people respected me. They made way for me when I walked down the street, and they stopped talking to let me speak. They hung on my every word. Everyone had good things to say about me. They commended me for all the people I had helped: the poor, orphans, widows, the blind, the lame, the needy, those without an advocate, and victims of evil.

"I assumed I would die peacefully as an old man, living a comfortable life in my home. At my funeral, people would praise me. But that hope is now gone.

"Unlike you three, when I would speak people would listen. They'd let me have the final word. They would seek out my advice and take it all in. Whenever I smiled at someone, they couldn't believe I gave them my attention. I led them as a king leads his army. And I comforted them when they mourned, a lesson you should take to heart now."

Though now enduring difficulty, Job recalls how people used to commend him:

- Job helped the poor. He responded when people asked for assistance. It's easy to come to the aid of friends, but what about strangers?

- Job supported orphans. God has a special place in his heart for the parentless. When we befriend orphans, we benefit them and honor God too.

- Job brought joy to widows. God also wants to protect widows. Though their plight today isn't as detrimental as it was then, we must still help widows in need.

- Job did what was right. The Bible calls this righteousness. By right living, we set an example for others and honor God.

- Job pursued justice. The marginalized long for fair treatment. We can come to their defense.

- Job became eyes for the blind. We should assist those who can't see and strive to make their life a bit easier.

- Job became feet to those who couldn't walk. We can also aid those who struggle to get around.

- Job was a father to those in need. To people who lack the necessities of life, we can be like a loving, gracious parent to support them.

- Job was an advocate. We can stand up for the oppressed and work to find them relief.
- Job opposed evil. Sin is everywhere. Do we ignore it or fight it?
- Job rescued the victims. When evil exists, victims result. We can rescue them.

This list is long, overwhelming. Jesus said we'll always have the poor with us, but that fact isn't an excuse to ignore them. We should do what we can to assist those around us.

What can we do to help one person today? What need can we commit ourselves to address for the long term?

[Discover more about helping others in Matthew 5:42, Luke 18:22, and James 1:27.]

DAY 29: WHEN GOD IS DISTANT
JOB 30

"I cry out to you, God, but you do not answer." Job 30:20

Having recalled how well people used to treat him and the respect they once gave him, Job contrasts that past to his present.

"How things have changed. Those who once praised me now mock me. They sing songs to ridicule me. They keep their distance as though they're afraid they might get what I've got. And when I get too close, they spit at me. Since God has removed his favor from me and made me weak, they don't hold back. They attack me and try to destroy me because they don't think anyone will come to my aid.

"I'm overwhelmed, existing in a constant state of terror. With my life receding, I'm about to die. My bones ache. Suffering grips me, and pain gnaws at my body. I plead with the Almighty for help, but he doesn't rescue me. He remains distant. Silent. He ignores me. Why has God turned against me?

"Why will no one offer me relief? I'm a broken man, crying out in distress. I have wept for others during their times of need. Will no one shed a tear for me now? I've hoped for good, but evil came. I sought light, but night overwhelmed me. The suffering in my gut will never go away. My misery knows no end. It's time to sing my funeral dirge."

As Job cries out from the anguish of his soul, he accuses others of turning their backs on him, of ignoring him, and of leaving him to suffer alone. Yes, friends and even family can be fickle, abandoning us when we need them most.

However, Job stops short of accusing the Almighty of these things. He merely laments that when he calls for help, God doesn't answer. He is distant, silent.

It's easy to feel close to God when times are good. But when hardship happens, we may not feel close to him. We may even believe that God abandoned us. This is how Job feels. In reading the book of Job, we may agree with him. Yet recall that God placed limits on Satan's ability to torment Job, requiring that the devil spare Job's life. Though God may not respond to Job's pleas in this season, God has not forgotten his servant and continues to protect him from death.

In our darkest times, do we turn to God or from him? When God doesn't seem to answer will we trust him anyway?

[Discover more about God's availability in Deuteronomy 31:6, Psalm 34:18, Matthew 28:20, James 4:8, and Revelation 3:20.]

DAY 30: IF . . . THEN

JOB 31

"Then these also would be sins to be judged, for I would have been unfaithful to God on high." Job 31:28

J
ob continues to share his despair.

"I pledged to never ogle a woman, because I thought God would notice and credit it to my account. After all, hardship befalls those who do bad, not good. Right?

"If I lied or deceived anyone, if I turned from God's path, or if I did what was wrong, then let others eat the crops I planted.

"If I allowed another woman to capture my attention, or if I sought my neighbor's wife, then may my spouse be given to another. For adultery is a wicked act, a sin worthy of judgment.

"If I denied anyone justice, if I refused to feed or clothe the poor, or if I oppressed orphans, then may my arms fall off. Even so, I fear God and would never forget to help others.

"If I placed my trust in my possessions, if I celebrated the money I've earned, or if I worshiped the sun and moon, then judge my sins for being unfaithful to the Lord God Almighty.

"If I celebrated other's troubles, if I failed to feed the hungry, or if I hid my sins because I was afraid of what other people would think . . . Oh, that someone would hear me and come to my defense . . . If my property accuses me of wrongdoing, or if I gathered my crops without paying my workers, then may weeds grow in my fields instead of wheat."

Job lets out a long sigh. He has nothing left to say. His shoulders drop, and his body crumples to the ground. Our camera pulls back and the image of Job blurs. The soundtrack softens to silence, and we fade to black.

Before Job wraps up his discourse, he mentions what he had done to avoid temptation, assuming God would honor him for it. He had tried to earn God's favor, but from Job's perspective, it didn't seem to work.

Job concludes with a series of if-then statements. Nineteen times he uses the word *if*. If he had done . . . followed by a list of sins that he could have committed. These various shortcomings cover a wide range of topics. Following each group of *if* statements, Job adds the word *then*, followed by the punishment he would accept.

Implicitly, he proclaims his innocence from all these things. He then rests his case before his friends and before God.

If we had to defend our integrity, would we have enough evidence? Do we think God owes us anything if we do good?

[Discover more about integrity in 1 Kings 9:4–5, Proverbs 10:9, Proverbs 11:3, Proverbs 13:6, and 2 Corinthians 1:12.]

DAY 31: ELIHU SPEAKS AT LAST
JOB 32–33

"For God does speak—now one way, now another—though no one perceives it." Job 33:14

J ob lies in a crumpled heap on the ground, ready to die. He waits for the Almighty to claim him. But one painful breath follows another. His time does not come. Ignoring his agony, he pushes his mind back to his children, not when they were young but his more recent picture of them celebrating life at the oldest one's home. But Job can't hold that image. Instead, his imagination pushes him forward to their horrific end. Our movie takes us to that scene.

Out of nowhere, rushing wind surrounds his children. Roaring. Raging. The house shakes. Debris falls from the ceiling. The main pillar cracks and disintegrates. With a mighty rumble, the roof caves in on his children. In an instant, they all die. Then everything becomes quiet.

Job relives the pain he felt when news of their death first reached him. Though he tries, he can't shake this ghastly thought from his memory.

The three men don't respond to Job's discourse —or to his silence. They remain mute, with the ash heap in front of them capturing their gaze. The fourth man, Elihu, who until now has stayed quiet, clears his throat. Though he lacks the grand trappings of the other three, he has a confident air that comes only from wealth and success. Elihu stands.

"Out of respect to my elders I remained quiet. But all this nonsense you're spouting compels me to speak. Job, you won't admit your faults. And you other three condemn him without evidence. How pathetic. Wisdom does not just come from age. Understanding also arises from the Spirit of God. Through him I will speak truth to you. May you listen.

"Job, you claim to be pure, a man without sin.

But you fail to state your case. You accuse God of treating you like his enemy. But you, my friend, are wrong.

"God is greater than any of us. You complain to him and say he doesn't answer. Despite what you claim, God does speak to us, in one way or another. If only we can perceive it. Dreams. Visions. Audible words. Angels. And he speaks through circumstances, just as you now endure.

"Pray to him and admit your faults. Then he will offer you mercy and rescue you from the pit that looms before you. He gives people opportunities to turn to him. Listen to me, Job, be silent and receive my wisdom."

Job claims that though he calls out to God, there's no answer. Elihu says God speaks through dreams, visions, circumstances, and audible words. Even through angels. It's up to us to perceive his message.

How does God speak to us? Are we open to hear from him regardless of how he reveals himself to us?

[Discover more about hearing from God in 1 Kings 19:12, Psalm 46:10, Matthew 13:15, James 1:22, and Revelation 2:29.]

DAY 32: ELIHU TALKS ABOUT JUSTICE

JOB 34–35

"It is unthinkable that God would do wrong, that the Almighty would pervert justice." Job 34:12

E lihu pauses, giving time for Job—or anyone else—to respond. When they don't, Elihu glances at the three older men and then resumes speaking.

"Listen to me, oh wise ones, as I continue. Weigh my words as I speak. May we work together to discern what is right, what is good.

"Job maintains his innocence and insists that God denies him justice. Job claims we treat him as a liar, even though he thinks it's useless to try to please God. However, the Almighty performs no evil. He does nothing wrong. He gives everyone what they deserve. No more no less. God governs us justly. Job doesn't know what he's talking about, and he piles rebellion on top of his sins.

"Job, by claiming you're right, you imply that God is wrong. Consider this: If you sin does that hurt God? If you do good does that benefit him? Of course not. Our actions only affect others— not God.

"The oppressed plead with the Almighty for relief, but they dare not question his integrity. God will not answer wicked people who cry out to him in arrogance. Think on this my friend. He ignores those who don't deserve his attention.

"Because of this truth, why do you expect he'll listen to you when you claim to not see him? When you present your case to him? When you find yourself waiting for an answer? You speak nonsense, Job. You say much, but it amounts to little."

Elihu perceives God as one who fairly administers justice but nothing more. Yes, we want God to act justly when it benefits us. But what about when it doesn't? Then we don't want justice. We want mercy. Mercy means not getting the bad results our actions demand.

Because we are frail people, we do wrong. We sin. If God *only* administers justice, then he must punish us for our mistakes. How fortunate for us that God is more than just. He is also merciful. In his mercy he gives us a way out. He provides Jesus. Jesus took upon himself the penalty that justice demanded for the wrongs we've committed. Jesus died so that we may live.

Have we accepted the solution Jesus offers as an alternative to the justice we deserve? Do we fully embrace Jesus for what he has done for us?

[Discover more about what Jesus did for us in John 3:16 and Romans 5:8.]

DAY 33: ELIHU SEES GOD IN NATURE
JOB 36–37

"How great is God—beyond our understanding!" Job 36:26

Elihu has worked himself into a frenzy. He pauses his tirade, and in one slow exhale he pushes the air out of his lungs as if expelling his agitation along with it. He closes his eyes to marshal the thoughts swirling around in his mind. When he opens his eyes, he sucks in a deep reserve of air and resumes his discourse.

"Please be patient with me a bit longer. I have more to say on God's behalf. He provides me with the knowledge that our Creator offers justice in all things. Rest assured that my words are true. You can count on the fact that I possess complete knowledge in this matter.

"God rewards those who are good and punishes those who do wrong. If only you would do what is right, then he will reward you again with prosperity like he did before. God yearns for you to turn to him, but you persist in pursuing evil. Now it's too late, and your punishment awaits."

A clap of distant thunder interrupts Elihu. After glancing at the dark skies that loom on the horizon, he continues.

"Through booming thunder, he proclaims that a gale draws near. With his hands he directs the lightning and guides the exploding shards of light to their targets. From the raging storm lightning flashes and thunder resounds. His voice echoes in the tempest. His words are too marvelous for us to understand. He accumulates rain in the clouds and dispenses it as he wishes to punish some people and bless others."

In a burst of brilliance, a flash of light shoots from the sky as it hurls toward the unsuspecting earth. Elihu smiles.

"Consider this, Job. Do you know how God makes lightning flash and thunder boom? Can you hold rain in the sky and direct its paths? Would you dare to stare into the sun when the clouds clear? In all this we see the immense majesty of God. He is beyond our grasp. We watch him rise, extolled by his great power. God is just. He is right. He does not oppress. Therefore, he deserves our attention."

Intermittent drops of water plop onto the dusty ground. The wind pushes the approaching storm closer. Its intensity increases as stinging rain pelts the men.

In this passage we see Elihu push forward in his arrogance that he has the knowledge his friends need. He repeats his view of God's justice and implies that Job is receiving the punishment he rightly deserves.

God directs the lightning and talks through the thunder. He governs the wind and sends the rain, giving to those he wishes to reward and devastating those he wishes to punish. All-powerful God commands our attention. He is worthy of our praise.

How can we worship God through nature? Can God speak to us through weather?

[Discover more about God's power in Genesis 1:31, Jonah 1:4, and Mark 4:39.]

DAY 34: SMACKDOWN
JOB 38:1–38

"Where were you when I laid the earth's foundation?" Job
38:4

The rain hurls to the ground in punishing sheets of water-filled pellets. The wind whips around the five men, threatening to blow them away. Thunder roars. Lightning explodes all around. They could scurry to shelter, but Job doesn't move. And the four men won't leave him. Though their words did not help him, they stay with him, loyal to the end, which may come soon.

Coming from the center of the storm, God speaks to Job.

"Who is this who dares to approach me in their ignorance? Brace yourself to hear my words. I have some questions for you, and then you must answer me—if you can.

"Were you there when I created the earth and the heavens? Did you help me plan how everything would fit together? Was it you who laid the earth's foundation and built upon it? What about the sun, moon, and stars?

"Can you control nature? Or even explain how it works? Consider the oceans, the clouds, and light itself. What about snow, hail, and lightning? Then there's the wind, rain, and thunder. Did you give birth to any of them?

"Look up in the night sky. Reflect on the stars and the constellations they form. Did you make them and set them in place? Do they answer to you?"

The book of Job uses thunder to characterize God. What a powerful metaphor.

Today, we have a technical understanding of thunder. But even though we understand thunder in a scientific way, it still produces an all-inspiring rumble that commands our attention.

Imagine how the ancient world viewed the roar of thunder: terrifying, powerful, unseen. It might parallel their comprehension of God.

Like thunder, God is both powerful and unseen. Who can understand him? Like thunder, God can have a booming loudness, terrifying. In contrast to this deafening intensity, God can also be a still small voice, a gentle whisper.

Job is in the middle of unimaginable turmoil, of unbearable pain. He has lost everything except for his breath and his faith—and both of those are tenuous. He seeks God for answers. This suffering man wants God to speak and explain why this has happened. He yearns to hear the voice of the Almighty, assuring him who's in control and that there's a purpose in all he has gone through.

Sometimes when God talks it's loud and other times it's soft. God can speak to us in diverse ways. These include through nature, friends, and circumstances, which is how he spoke to Job.

Regardless of how God speaks, he does speak to us. We must prepare ourselves to hear what he has to say.

When God speaks, are we ready to listen? Are we open to hear him in ways that we might not have considered before?

[Discover more about God speaking to his people in Genesis 15:1, Exodus 3:4, Matthew 2:12, Luke 2:26, Acts 16:6, Hebrews 1:1–2, and Hebrews 4:12.]

DAY 35: GOD'S AWE-INSPIRING CREATION

JOB 38:39–39:30

"Does the eagle soar at your command and build its nest on high?" Job 39:27

As the storm's intensity increases, Job's four friends cast wary glances at each other, interspersed with worried peeks at the raging weather. They give longing gazes at the shelter Job's nearby house affords. But Job sits unfazed amid the storm's fury. Unmoved.

None of the friends wants to surrender first, to dash to shelter and leave Job alone. More light flashes. More reverberations. God continues to speak.

"Do you guide the lioness to food as she hunts?

Or feed the raven as she strives to care for her hatchlings? Do you know when the mountain goats give birth or watch the doe's fawn emerge? Have you set the wild donkeys free or provided them with a place to live? Can you control the wild ox?

"Consider the ways of the ostrich and the stork. Did you make each of them different? Do you give the horse its strength and speed? Do the hawks and eagles fly, hunt, and nest at your command?"

For all that we know about the animals God created, there's so much that exceeds our comprehension. Each species has its unique characteristics, some amazing in their complexity (how a snake slithers or a hummingbird flies), others frustrating in their limitations (sheep are dumb), and still others are humorous in their behavior (witness the otter at play or how a hen strides).

Some animals walk, others fly. A few do both, though they usually excel at one over the other. Some animals lay eggs while others birth their young. Among the animal kingdom we see great diversity.

As people, we also carry our own uniqueness, with each person different from every other. There are no two of us alike. Everyone has their own inherent strengths and weaknesses. Still God cares for us all. He loves us and wants to be in relationship with us, regardless of who we are or what we've done.

Do we desire to be in relationship with our Creator? How can God's amazing creation draw us to him and provoke us into holy worship of our Maker?

[Discover more about God's creation in Genesis 1:27, Genesis 1:31, 2 Corinthians 5:17, and Hebrews 4:13.]

DIG DEEPER: THE MOVIE SECRETARIAT

"Do you give the horse its strength or clothe its neck with a flowing mane?" Job 39:19

From the movie *Secretariat* come these lines:

Do you give the horse its strength or clothe its neck with a flowing mane? Do you make it leap like a locust, striking terror with its proud snorting? It paws fiercely, rejoicing in its strength, and charges into the fray. It laughs at fear, afraid of nothing; it does not shy away from the sword. The quiver rattles against its side, along with the flashing spear and lance. In frenzied excitement it eats up the ground; it cannot stand still when the trumpet sounds.

Although this is an apt description of the mighty steed Secretariat, it isn't about him—not really. This passage wasn't written for the movie. It originated a few millennia before. It comes from the book of Job.

The movie quotes directly from the NIV Bible, Job 39:19–24. They are God's words to Job, reminding Job of God's creative genius. If he cares so much for the animals he made, how much more he must esteem us.

What can we learn from the movie Secretariat? *Do we see God's awe-inspiring ingenuity in the animals he created?*

[Discover more about horses in 2 Kings 2:11, Esther 8:10, James 3:3, and Revelation 19:14.]

DAY 36: CONTENDING WITH GOD AND CORRECTING HIM

JOB 40:1–14

"I am unworthy—how can I reply to you? I put my hand over my mouth." Job 40:4

The storm that God whipped up continues, though its intensity lessens. The downpour changes from a torrent to a cleansing shower. The gale eases its assault, morphing into a stiff breeze. The soaked friends shiver. Their drenched clothes have lost their regal air. Rubbing water from their faces, they look not at Job or the saturated ash pile in front of them. Instead, they fix their gaze at the center of the retreating storm, as if looking at God himself and giving him their complete attention.

They don't need to wait long for God to continue speaking. "Though you contend with me, do you think you can correct me?"

After a long delay, Job opens his mouth. In barely a whisper, he forces out a raspy response. "I'm completely unworthy to answer. Though I've spoken once and then twice, I'll now keep my mouth shut."

"Be a man. Get ready to answer me," God says. "I have questions for you, and I expect a response. Who are you to accuse me of injustice? Why must you pull me down to elevate yourself?

"Do you have the strength that I have? Are you as powerful as me? If so, then act like a god to humble the proud and punish the wicked. Send them to their grave. If you can do that, then I'll admit that you're able to save yourself."

Job doesn't answer, at least not yet.

Let's recap. Job's life has crumbled. His wife has turned on him. And his friends don't help. After listening to their back-and-forth discourse that accomplishes nothing, God interjects. At last he speaks.

God asks Job a rhetorical question with two

concepts. The first is the idea of contending with God, and the second is correcting him.

Though we could view God's question as implying that he doesn't want us to contend with him, that's not what he means. *Contend* means to debate or struggle. When it comes to God, these are strong words. It seems foolish for us to debate God, to struggle with him. God is sovereign. We aren't. Who are we to question his decisions?

But I don't recall any place in the Bible where God punishes his people for contending with him, providing they do so with reverence. I can't find a single verse that commands us to not question God or debate his ways. Instead, he seems to enjoy when we ask questions—serious, soul-wrenching questions —just like Job.

However, there's a right way to contend with God and a wrong way. The wrong way is when we think we know better than him, when we try to correct him and tell him he's wrong, that he made a mistake. This would be an error on our part.

Though it may be okay to contend with God in a respectful way, we shouldn't try to correct him. Doing so would attempt to elevate ourselves over him. Though God enjoys our sincere questions, we must never forget our place, that he is our sovereign Creator and we are his creation.

How willing are we to contend with God? How can we question God in a respectful way?

[Discover more about people who contended with God in Genesis 18:20–33, Exodus 32:9–14, 2 Kings 20:1–6, and Luke 22:42–44.]

DAY 37: THE BEHEMOTH AND LEVIATHAN

JOB 40:15–41:34

"Who then is able to stand against me?" Job 41:10

Job considers the words God spoke to him. The Almighty has made his point. Clarity emerges. Though not rebuked for contending with his Maker, Job realizes he overstepped in accusing God of being unjust, in trying to correct God for perceived errors.

Though God insists that Job answer him, Job has no response. Words are inadequate. Job stays quiet. In a way, saying nothing *is* his answer. When standing repentant before our all-powerful, sovereign Lord, silence may be the best response.

God resumes his instruction. "Consider

Behemoth. I made him when I made you. Look at his strength and his power. There is no one in all my creation that matches him. He prevails first among all creatures. He fears nothing, and no one can capture him.

"Or consider Leviathan. Who can oppose him? Attempts to catch him always fail. He laughs at those who pursue him. Who would dare try to corral him or turn him into a pet? No one can subdue him, and he overpowers all who approach.

"Remember, I created Leviathan. If you can't stand against him, how dare you think you can stand against me. I made the heavens and the earth. I placed you here. All belongs to me. What claim can you make against me that I must repay?"

God continues talking about the mighty power and immense strength of Leviathan. "He terrifies all who cross his paths. Nothing is his equal. He exists without fear, looking down on the arrogant. He reigns over everything."

God wraps up his rebuttal to Job and his friends by talking about two awe-inspiring creatures: the behemoth and the leviathan.

This is the only place where the Bible mentions

Behemoth. It could be a generic reference to a large beast or the name of a specific species. Though it could be a mythological creature, it's more likely that Behemoth was a real animal, one either now extinct or still living among us. Bible scholars offer suggestions for this mighty animal. These include elephant, rhinoceros, water buffalo, hippopotamus, or even brontosaurus. Regardless, Behemoth is a powerful animal that we don't want to contend with.

Next is Leviathan. We already covered him in "Dig Deeper: What's a Leviathan?" Likewise, a leviathan could be a mythological creature, a beast now extinct, or an animal that's still with us. Some Bible scholars wonder if Leviathan could be an ancestor of today's crocodile—a giant crocodile, if you will. Regardless of what Leviathan is, no one wants to mess with one.

What we don't want to miss, however, is that in the middle of talking about these powerful creatures, God asks Job—and us—a powerful question. "Given that you can't stand up against these beasts, why do you think you can stand up against me, the one who made them?"

Since we fear things here on earth, we should fear, even more so, Almighty God.

How do we understand having a healthy fear of God? How do we balance fearing God with loving him?

[Discover more about fearing God in Genesis 22:12, Psalm 66:16, Ecclesiastes 12:13, and 1 Peter 2:17. Read more about loving God in 1 Corinthians 8:3 and 1 John 4:7–21.]

DAY 38: JOB'S CONFESSION
JOB 42:1–6

"I spoke of things I did not understand, things too wonderful for me to know." Job 42:3

The rain stops. The sun comes out. Its warm brilliance soothes everything that the storm soaked. Job's four friends peel off their sopping wet robes and drenched turbans, wringing water from them as the sun dries their dripping-wet bodies and soothes their shivering skin. Though cold and shaking, Job doesn't follow their lead. Instead, he raises his arms toward the sky and looks upward as if peering into the eyes of God.

"I realize now, Lord, that you're all-powerful. No one can prevent your will from finding its complete fulfillment. You have asked me a question for which I have no answer. In all humility, let me admit that I spoke in ignorance of things I didn't know, of things too amazing for me to understand.

"But I did listen. I heard every word you said. I saw your face as you spoke. I am nothing compared to you. I hate myself for what I thought and what I said. I humble myself before you as I sit repentant here in this heap of ashes."

Job lowers his arms and drops his gaze from heaven above to the drenched ashes before him. He leans forward and touches his forehead to the muddy cinders. Falling prostrate before Almighty God, Job stills himself in humble adoration before his Lord.

A common lament of Job throughout this story is his begging God to answer his pleas. However, it seems Job (and his friends) are too busy spouting off about God to give him a chance to respond. When God does speak, he rebuffs Job's friends and affirms Job's righteousness.

Job's brief reply to God's discourse is contrite. After acknowledging God's complete knowledge (omniscience) and total power (omnipotence), Job admits that his words exceeded his understanding.

With all our insight about God and our assumed comprehension of his ways, we must be careful to not make the same mistake as Job and his friends. We run the risk of spouting our religious opinions—our theology—with assured confidence as if they were fact. A more likely reality when we do this is that we speak of things we don't understand.

Fortunately, we serve a forgiving God, one who is benevolent and not malevolent. He offers us mercy when we don't deserve it and doesn't demand the justice our actions warrant.

How have we used our understanding of God—our theology —in ways that hurt others? How can we better treat others by offering mercy and not demanding justice?

[Discover more about knowledge in Psalm 119:66 and 1 Corinthians 8:1. Read more about mercy versus justice in Amos 5:15, Zechariah 7:9, and Matthew 23:23.]

DIG DEEPER: THREE LESSONS FROM JOB

If any of you lacks wisdom, you should ask God, who gives generously to all without finding fault, and it will be given to you. James 1:5

Here are three thoughts from the book of Job.

First, what Job fears most is what happened to him. The enemy (that is Satan, the devil) knew Job's fears and exploited them. Although everyone fears something, we should turn our fears over to God and not dwell on them. Holding on to our fears gives the enemy an obvious way to attack us.

Next, Job believes that through good behavior

he deserves God's blessings. Things aren't any different today. The common belief is that we can earn God's love, that our efforts to do good will merit his attention.

Of course, we are quick to reject the opposite. People assume that their wrong actions should receive forgiveness, not punishment. The right motivation for good behavior is simply as a response to what God has already done for us. We do good things out of respect for God and to honor him, not to earn something in return.

Last, and most important, when Job has nothing left to say and stops talking, that is when God speaks. It's hard for us to listen to others when we're talking. It's no different in our relationship with God.

When we pray, do we spend more time talking or listening? In what ways can we better turn our fears over to God?

[Discover more about these three thoughts in Psalm 55:22, Ephesians 2:8–9, and Psalm 46:10.]

DAY 39: GOD CRITICIZES JOB'S FRIENDS

JOB 42:7–9

"I am angry with you and your two friends, because you have not spoken the truth about me, as my servant Job has." Job 42:7

Our camera zooms in on Job for a close-up. He stays bowed in humble worship before his Lord. God has finished speaking to his servant, but he still has a final message for Job's three friends. (God doesn't address Elihu, neither affirming nor criticizing his words.)

"I'm angry at you Eliphaz, along with your two friends. Though Job spoke truth about me, you three failed to do so. You deserve punishment for your errors. You must present a sacrifice to atone for your mistakes. And after you make your burnt offerings, Job will pray for you. I'll accept his prayers and forgive you for your foolishness."

The three men—Eliphaz, Bildad, and Zophar —offer a sacrifice of seven bulls and seven rams as God instructed. Then Job prays they'll receive God's forgiveness, and God accepts Job's request.

After Job's supposed friends fail so miserably to comfort him in his time of need, after they malign him, God steps in. He puts them in their place for what they said, and he affirms that Job has spoken truth.

Imagine the situation. Job's life is in shambles. He's destitute and in pain, despising life itself. The only people who will even talk to him attack his character, pulling him down even further. Then, after their hurtful words, they have the audacity to expect him to pray for them.

If we were Job, how would we respond?

Praying for them would be a most challenging task. I suspect we'd find it far easier to want those friends to receive the payback they deserve for their wrong counsel. But not Job. Amid his torment, he prays for his misguided friends, even though they seem to be in a much better state than he is.

Notice that God doesn't tell Job to pray for his errant friends after they offer their sacrifice. What if Job decides not to intervene for them? After how they failed to support him, we'd understand if he snubbed them and let God deal with them as they deserve.

However, God knows Job. He knows Job's heart. He knows Job will pray for these men even though they let him down.

And God says he will accept Job's prayer. Before Job utters the words, God promises to honor what his follower *will* pray. What an affirmation of Job's godly character and God's esteem for him.

May our relationship with God be like Job's, with hearts so attuned to our Lord that he says "yes" before we even say "please."

How do we think God perceives our prayers? Do we expect he'll answer when we pray?

[Discover more about prayer in 1 Chronicles 4:10, Matthew 6:5–6, James 5:15, and Jude 1:20.]

DAY 40: JOB'S OUTCOME
JOB 42:10–16

The Lord restored his fortunes and gave him twice as much as he had before. Job 42:10

At this point in our movie, God has affirmed Job and restored his friends' status after reprimanding them and receiving Job's prayer. Now we have a final scene to conclude our story. Despite all that's happened, Job's situation hasn't changed. Satan has stripped him of everything: his family, his wealth, and his health. And despite having prayed for his friends, Job persists in his position of prostrate reverence before God.

With the storm having passed and nice weather

returning, the music in our soundtrack swells. A bright beam of sunlight illuminates the area where Job lays in contrite submission. As he struggles to rise before his maker, fighting to overcome the pain of his broken body, God's blessings begin to flow to Job.

By the time Job stands fully erect, confident and whole, we see—through cinematic magic—that God has returned all that Satan took away, times two. A double portion. Job's extended family returns, giving him gifts and encouragement. His flocks number twice what he had before. God blesses him with ten more children.

The scene of Job, smiling broadly in the middle of his restored prosperity, gets brighter and brighter until the image washes out to a heavenly white. Then we read a final epilogue on the screen:

After all this Job lived 140 years. He celebrated life with his children, grandchildren, great-grandchildren, and great-great-grandchildren. He enjoyed a full and meaningful life.

Fade to black. Roll credits.

After Job prays, God restores his fortunes twofold. What if Job had refused to pray for his friends? Might God's response have been different?

God restores to Job what Satan took away. God doubles Job's wealth and gives him ten more kids: seven sons and three daughters.

Though the Bible doesn't record the sons' names, it does list the daughters: Jemimah, Keziah, and Keren-Happuch. In an age when society revered sons and diminished daughters, righteous Job elevates his girls. Even more so, Job goes against the practice of the day, giving his daughters an inheritance along with their brothers.

This is a counter-cultural move—and one that must delight God. In doing so, Job reveals his heart and God's perspective. This is even more remarkable, given that Job lives in a male-dominated society.

May we follow Job's example in our lives.

How can we better align our heart with God's perspective? What can we do to elevate the status of those whom society has pushed down?

[Discover more about God's heart in Psalm 146:7–8, Isaiah 58:5–7, and Isaiah 61:1–3.]

If you liked *Job Bible Study*, please leave a review online. Your review will help others discover this book and encourage them to read it too.

Thank you.

FOR SMALL GROUPS, SUNDAY SCHOOL, AND CLASSES

Job Bible Study makes an ideal eight-week Bible study discussion guide for small groups, Sunday School, and classes. To prepare for the conversation, read one chapter of this book each weekday, Monday through Friday.

- Week 1: read 1 through 5.
- Week 2: read 6 through 10.
- Week 3: read 11 through 15.
- Week 4: read 16 through 20.
- Week 5: read 21 through 25.
- Week 6: read 26 through 30.
- Week 7: read 31 through 35.
- Week 8: read 36 through 40.

When you get together, discuss the questions at the end of each chapter. The leader can use all the questions to guide this discussion or pick which ones to focus on.

Before beginning the discussion, pray as a group. Ask for Holy Spirit insight and clarity.

As you consider each chapter's questions:

- Look for how this can grow your understanding of the Bible.
- Evaluate how this can expand your faith perspective.
- Consider what you need to change in how you live your lives.

End by asking God to help apply what you've learned.

May God bless you as you read and study his Word.

IF YOU'RE NEW TO THE BIBLE

Each entry in this book contains Bible references. These can guide you if you want to learn more. If you're not familiar with the Bible, here's an overview to get you started, give some context, and minimize confusion.

First, the Bible is a collection of works written by various authors over several centuries. Think of the Bible as a diverse anthology of godly communication. It contains historical accounts, poetry, songs, letters of instruction and encouragement, messages from God sent through his representatives, and prophecies.

Most versions of the Bible have sixty-six books grouped into two sections: The Old Testament and the New Testament. The Old Testament contains thirty-nine books that precede and anticipate Jesus. The New Testament includes twenty-seven books and covers Jesus's life and the work of his followers.

The reference notations in the Bible, such as Romans 3:23, are analogous to line numbers in a Shakespearean play. They serve as a study aid. Since the Bible is much longer and more complex than a play, its reference notations are more involved.

As already mentioned, the Bible is an amalgam of books, or sections, such as Genesis, Matthew, or Acts. These are the names given to them, over time, based on the piece's author, audience, or purpose.

In the 1200s, each book was divided into chapters, such as Acts 2 or Psalm 23. In the 1500s, the chapters were further subdivided into verses, such as John 3:16. Let's use this as an example.

The name of the book (John) appears first, followed by the chapter number (3), a colon, and then the verse number (16). Sometimes called a chapter-verse reference notation, this helps people quickly find a specific text regardless of their version of the Bible.

Although the goal was to place these chapter and verse divisions at logical breaks, they sometimes seem arbitrary. Therefore, it's good practice to read what precedes and follows each passage you're studying. The text before or after it may contain relevant insights into the portion you're exploring.

Here's how to look up a specific passage in the Bible based on its reference: Most Bibles contain a table of contents, which gives the page number for the beginning of each book. Start there. Locate the book you want to read, and turn to that page. Then flip forward to the chapter you want. Last, skim that chapter to locate the specific verse.

If you want to read online, enter the reference into BibleGateway.com or BibleHub.com. Also check out the YouVersion app.

Learn more about the greatest book ever written at ABibleADay.com, which provides a Bible blog, summaries of the books of the Bible, a dictionary of Bible terms, Bible reading plans, and other resources.

ABOUT PETER DEHAAN

Peter DeHaan, PhD, wants to change the world one word at a time. His books and blog posts discuss God, the Bible, and church, geared toward spiritual seekers and church dropouts. Many people feel church has let them down, and Peter seeks to encourage them as they search for a place to belong.

But he's not afraid to ask tough questions or make religious people squirm. He's not trying to be provocative. Instead, he seeks truth, even if it makes people uncomfortable. Peter urges Christians to push past the status quo and reexamine how they practice their faith in every part of their lives.

Peter earned his doctorate, awarded with high distinction, from Trinity College of the Bible and Theological Seminary. He lives with his wife in beautiful Southwest Michigan and wrangles crossword puzzles in his spare time.

A lifelong student of Scripture, Peter wrote the 1,000-page website ABibleADay.com to encourage people to explore the Bible, the greatest book ever written. His popular blog, at PeterDeHaan.com, addresses biblical Christianity to build a faith that matters.

Read his blog, receive his newsletter, and learn more at PeterDeHaan.com.

BOOKS BY PETER DEHAAN

40-Day Bible Study Series

Dear Theophilus (the Gospel of Luke)

Acts Bible Study

Isaiah Bible Study

Dear Theophilus, Minor Prophets

Living Water (John)

Love Is Patient (1 and 2 Corinthians)

Revelation Bible Study

Love One Another (1, 2, and 3 John)

Run with Perseverance (Hebrews)

James and Jude Bible Study

Matthew Bible Study

1 & 2 Peter Bible Study

Mark Bible Study

Holiday Celebration Devotionals

The Advent of Jesus

The Passion of Jesus (Lent)

The Victory of Jesus (Easter)

The Ministry of Jesus

Thanksgiving with Jesus

Bible Character Sketches Series

Women of the Bible

The Friends and Foes of Jesus

Old Testament Sinners and Saints

More Old Testament Sinners and Saints

Heroes and Heavies of the Apocrypha

200 Old Testament Sinners and Saints

Visiting Churches Series

52 Churches

The 52 Churches Workbook

More Than 52 Churches

The More Than 52 Churches Workbook

Visiting Online Church

Shopping for Church

Other Books

Elephant God

Jesus's Broken Church

Martin Luther's 95 Theses (formerly *95 Tweets*)

The Christian Church's LGBTQ Failure

Bridging the Sacred-Secular Divide (formerly *Woodpecker Wars*)

Beyond Psalm 150

How Big Is Your Tent?

For the latest list of all Peter's books, go to PeterDeHaan.com/books.